D1310704

THE
John
PROJECT

The Gospel of Jesus Christ,
as Written by the Apostle John,
with a Guide to Reading and
Learning the Word of God

1941
PUBLISHING™

© Young Life Discipleship

Published by 1941 Publishing™
a division of Young Life Discipleship
Young Life, P.O. Box 540, Colorado Springs, CO 80901

discipleship.younglife.org
discipleship@sc.younglife.org

Printed in the United States of America

Senior Editor: Crystal Kirgiss
Layout and Design: Isaac Watkins
Copy Editor: Jessica Williams
Tiny Devo Contributors: Marisa Avramovich, Julie Clapp, Beth Griebel, Carolyn Harrison, Kelsey Jenney, Crystal Kirgiss, Sean McGever, Ken Tankersley, Aretta Zitta

Proceeds from the sale of this book will be used to help fund future 1941 Publishing discipleship projects.

(Use this page to test different pens, pencils, highlighters, or markers to see which ones work OK in this book.)

Contents

HOW TO
Read
THIS BOOK

HOW TO
Read
THIS BOOK

This book should be read several times, in several ways.

1. Start with The BIG Story on pages 12 and 13. It tells a quick version of God's Word up to the time of Jesus.

2. Read John — left-hand pages only, starting on page 18 — from beginning to end. Don't worry about understanding all the details. Just read the whole story over the course of a week. You can write questions or thoughts in the left-hand margin as you go.

3. Next watch the two BibleProject videos about John. You'll find URLs and QR codes on page 15.

4. Then read John again from beginning to end, but this time do the things on the right-hand pages as you go. Don't worry about doing this quickly. Go at a comfortable pace, allowing time to think, wonder, consider, and learn.

5. Finally, read John one more time from beginning to end, focusing on just the left-hand pages. Use the list of Margin Icons on page 15 to help identify important ideas and themes as you read. Draw the relevant icon in the left-hand margins.

In the book of John on the left-hand pages, the words of Jesus are in *italics*.

The right-hand pages have eight sections. The next page explains those.

FYI

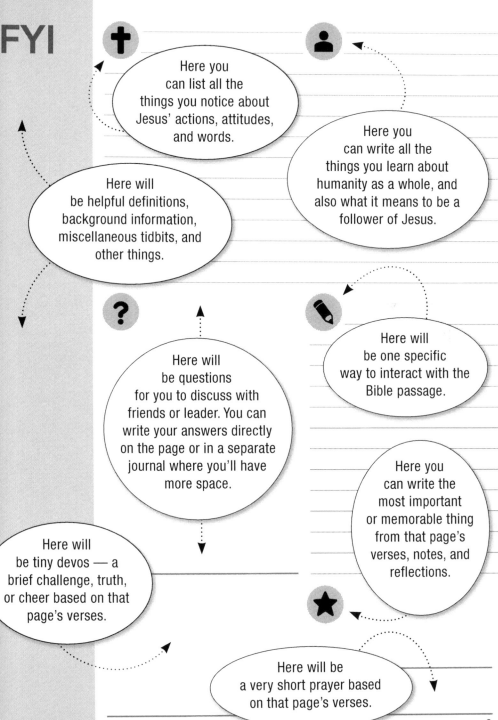

Here you can list all the things you notice about Jesus' actions, attitudes, and words.

Here you can write all the things you learn about humanity as a whole, and also what it means to be a follower of Jesus.

Here will be helpful definitions, background information, miscellaneous tidbits, and other things.

Here will be questions for you to discuss with friends or leader. You can write your answers directly on the page or in a separate journal where you'll have more space.

Here will be one specific way to interact with the Bible passage.

Here you can write the most important or memorable thing from that page's verses, notes, and reflections.

Here will be tiny devos — a brief challenge, truth, or cheer based on that page's verses.

Here will be a very short prayer based on that page's verses.

THE Big STORY

Big THE
STORY

The story of God starts like this:

Genesis 1:1   **In the beginning God created the heavens and the earth.**

Genesis 1:31   The story started out very good. God said so himself. But humanity, God's special
                   and beloved creation, quickly spoiled things by rejecting the identity and the
Genesis 3   responsibility God had given them. Translation: they rejected God himself.

                   It would have been fair for God to reject humanity in return. But he didn't.
Genesis 12-50   Instead, he chose a specific family (Abraham, father of Isaac, father of Jacob
                   — also known as Israel) to live as his people and to share his truth with all the
                   nations.

                   Except they didn't. They failed miserably.

Exodus   At one point they were enslaved in Egypt for hundreds of years. Eventually they
Numbers   were led to freedom by a man named Moses. But on their journey to a new home,
Deuteronomy   they messed up again and again. When they finally arrived in the Promised Land
                   40 years later, God gave them leaders called judges (not like our modern judges),
Joshua   some of whom did a good job and some of whom failed miserably.
Judges

1 – 2 Samuel   One day, God's people said, "No more judges. We want a king, like all the other
                   nations have," forgetting that they already had a King — God himself. Once
                   again, God had every right to reject the people who'd rejected him. But he didn't.
                   He gave them what they asked for. A few of the kings did a good job. Most of
                   them failed miserably. The most important king was David. God promised David
                   that someday one of his descendants would reign over God's people forever.

1 – 2 Kings   Next failure: God's chosen nation split into a northern nation (Israel) and a
1 – 2 Chronicles southern nation (Judah). Bigger and stronger nations began attacking them. God
Isaiah   sent prophets — people who spoke on God's behalf — to warn about the results
Jeremiah   of disobedience and unfaithfulness. The kings and the people mostly ignored the
Ezekiel   prophets and rejected God's warnings.
Hosea-Malachi

2 Kings 17   Israel (capital city: Samaria) was defeated first. The people were exiled to the
                   conquering nation, Assyria. They never returned home.

2 Kings 25   Judah (capital city: Jerusalem) held on for another 150 years. But eventually they were conquered too. The sacred Temple was destroyed. Most people were exiled to the conquering nation, Babylon. They cried out for justice and rescue.

Nehemiah   Generations later, some exiles were allowed to return home. They began to rebuild the city walls and the Temple. But life was difficult. The people cried out to God. God promised that someday a Messiah would come to rescue his people, restore the Temple, and establish a new Kingdom.

Between the Old and New Testaments   For 400 years, powers kept shifting. Judah, or Judea, was ruled by Persians, then Greeks, and finally Romans. The Jewish people kept waiting and hoping for the promised Messiah to arrive, restore their nation, and defeat their enemies. They hoped for a strong and mighty leader who would drive out the Romans, sit on the throne as king, and welcome God back to a bigger and better Temple. They waited. And waited. And waited some more. Some would-be messiahs appeared, but all turned out to be imposters.

Matthew
Mark
Luke
John   And then Jesus was born. And lived. And died. And rose again.

And a man named John — one of Jesus' closest friends — wrote down what had happened.

The story he wrote starts like this:
John 1:1   **In the beginning the Word already existed. The Word was with God, and the Word was God.**

John's story is connected to The Big Story. But although The Big Story began "very good" and went downhill from there, when Jesus appeared on the scene, things began returning to the "very good" that God originally intended.

This is that story.

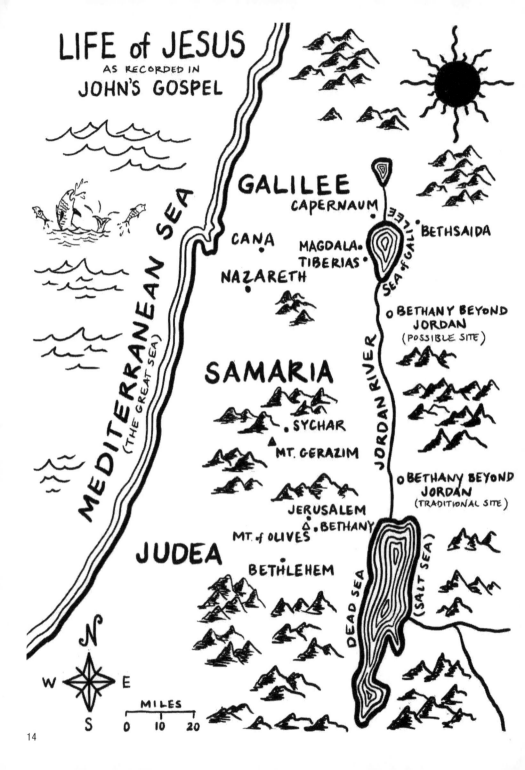

Margin Icons

♛ Kingdom / King / Messiah

† crucifixion

⟊ resurrection

↓♡ God's love for us

↑♡ our love for God

←♡ our love for others

◉ abide / Christ in you

H S Holy Spirit

o O disciple / discipleship

↻ repentance

◖ forgiveness / washed clean

↑ faith / belief

✬ obedience / new life

✗ disobedience / sin / old life

↕ prayer

☼ light

♍ spiritual fruit

‿ joy

Some Helpful Things

 BibleProject John 1-12
https://bibleproject.com/explore/
video/john-1-12/

 AUDIO BIBLE
Full New Testament (NIV) with a
hip-hop soundtrack
https://www.streetlightsbible.com

 BibleProject John 13-21
https://bibleproject.com/explore/
video/john-13-21/

DAILY MINI-DEVOS
An Instagram morsel of challenge, truth, and
cheer @yl_discipleship

 BIBLE READING PLANS
Five-Day Bible App Reading Plans
(read on your own or in a virtual
group) https://discipleship.
younglife.org/bible-app/

John

The Gospel of Jesus Christ, as Written by the Apostle John,
with a Guide to Reading and Learning the Word of God

The Good News According to John

CHAPTER 1 In the beginning the Word already existed.

The Word was with God,

and the Word was God.

2 He existed in the beginning with God.

3 God created everything through him,

and nothing was created except through him.

4 The Word gave life to everything that was created,

and his life brought light to everyone.

5 The light shines in the darkness,

and the darkness can never extinguish it.

6 God sent a man, John the Baptist, 7 to tell about the light so that everyone might believe because of his testimony. 8 John himself was not the light; he was simply a witness to tell about the light. 9 The one who is the true light, who gives light to everyone, was coming into the world.

10 He came into the very world he created, but the world didn't recognize him. 11 He came to his own people, and even they rejected him. 12 But to all who believed him and accepted him, he gave the right to become children of God. 13 They are reborn–not with a physical birth resulting from human passion or plan, but a birth that comes from God.

14 So the Word became human and made his home among us. He was full of unfailing love and faithfulness. And we have seen his glory, the glory of the Father's one and only Son.

15 John testified about him when he shouted to the crowds, "This is the one I was talking about when I said, 'Someone is coming after me who is far greater than I am, for he existed long before me.'"

16 From his abundance we have all received one gracious blessing after another. 17 For the law was given through Moses, but God's unfailing love and faithfulness came through Jesus Christ. 18 No one has ever seen God. But the unique One, who is himself God, is near to the Father's heart. He has revealed God to us.

FYI

Why do you think John begins as he does (verses 1-5) instead of with the Christmas story?

What do you think it means to believe and accept Jesus (verse 12)?

How has Jesus helped you know and understand God, or "revealed God to you" (verse 18)?

Copy verses 4 and 5 here.

John starts just like the first verse of the Bible, Genesis 1:1 – "In the beginning God created the heavens and the earth."

Moses led the Israelites — also known as the Hebrew people — out of slavery in Egypt to a new land of their own. That story is retold (with some changes) in the movie The Prince of Egypt.

"The law" was a collection of teachings and guidelines for the Israelites about how to live the way God intended for humanity. Some of the laws were temporary, like what kind of food to eat, what type of fabric clothes should be made from, and what special days to celebrate. Some of the laws were lasting, like how we treat others, the importance of honesty, loving God with our whole selves, and more. Jesus teaches about what laws are still in play.

Jesus Christ isn't a first and last name. It's a first name and a descriptive title. Jesus is a personal name, which was "Yeshua" in the original language. Christ is another word for Messiah, which is an ancient word for anointed one or King. These all mean the same thing: Jesus Christ; Jesus the Christ; Jesus the Messiah; Jesus the anointed one; Jesus the King; King Jesus.

Sometimes the world feels like a very dark place, full of worry, pain, suffering, lies, and hatred. Jesus is the LIGHT OF THE WORLD. He shatters darkness by bringing hope, rest, comfort, guidance, truth, and love. Jesus the Light is always there — even when it's hard to see, hear, and feel. Choose to live in the Light today. Let it guide you, comfort you, and wrap you in its love. (John 1:5)

Dear God — Please help me learn more about you as I read the Bible.

*Testimony of
John the Baptist*

19 This was John's testimony when the Jewish leaders sent priests and Temple assistants from Jerusalem to ask John, "Who are you?" 20 He came right out and said, "I am not the Messiah."

21 "Well then, who are you?" they asked. "Are you Elijah?"

"No," he replied.

"Are you the Prophet we are expecting?

"No."

22 "Then who are you? We need an answer for those who sent us. What do you have to say about yourself?"

23 John replied in the words of the prophet Isaiah:

"I am a voice shouting in the wilderness,
'Clear the way for the Lord's coming!'"

24 Then the Pharisees who had been sent 25 asked him, "If you aren't the Messiah or Elijah or the Prophet, what right do you have to baptize?"

26 John told them, "I baptize with water, but right here in the crowd is someone you do not recognize. 27 Though his ministry follows mine, I'm not even worthy to be his slave and untie the straps of his sandal."

28 This encounter took place in Bethany, an area east of the Jordan River, where John was baptizing.

*Jesus, the
Lamb of God*

29 The next day John saw Jesus coming toward him and said, "Look! The Lamb of God who takes away the sin of the world! 30 He is the one I was talking about when I said, 'A man is coming after me who is far greater than I am, for he existed long before me.' 31 I did not recognize him as the Messiah, but I have been baptizing with water so that he might be revealed to Israel."

32 Then John testified, "I saw the Holy Spirit descending like a dove from heaven and resting upon him. 33 I didn't know he was the one, but when God sent me to baptize with water, he told me, 'The one on whom you see the Spirit descend and rest is the one who will baptize with the Holy Spirit.' 34 I saw this happen to Jesus, so I testify that he is the Chosen One of God."

FYI

Jerusalem was the capital city of Judea. The Temple, the center of Jewish religion, was in Jerusalem.

Prophets were people in the Old Testament who spoke God's truth to the people.

Elijah was an Old Testament prophet who delivered God's messages to the nation of Israel. His story is in 1 Kings 17-19. The Old Testament ends with a promise that a powerful prophet like Elijah would come again someday. (Malachi 4:5)

In verse 23, John the Baptist quotes another Old Testament prophet, **Isaiah.** *(Isaiah 40:3)*

Pharisees had been around for 200 years before the time of Jesus. They were dedicated to carefully keeping all the Jewish laws and traditions so that their religion and culture weren't weakened or watered down.

John the Baptist was Jesus' second cousin. His mother (Elizabeth) and Jesus' mother (Mary) were cousins. That story is found in Luke 1.

Messiah is the Hebrew word for "Anointed One." **Christ** is the Greek translation. The Jewish people had been waiting hundreds of years for the promised Messiah to come and rescue them from their enemies.

 Where did you first hear about Jesus? Who was speaking about him? Why did you listen and believe?

Why do you think people listened to and believed what John the Baptist was saying?

 List all the things John says he isn't.

List all the things John says Jesus is.

How would you describe John's attitude and view of himself?

Even though we weren't there when Jesus lived and walked on earth as a human being, and even though we didn't meet him face-to-face in the flesh, and even though we haven't sat at his actual feet listening to him teach, followers of Jesus today can still "testify that Jesus is the Chosen One of God," just like John the Baptist did (see verse 34). We do this by living as he taught us to, by sharing what we've experienced, and by speaking truth about Jesus Christ.

Dear God — Thank you for sending your son, Jesus, to "take away the sin of the world!" (John 1:29)

The First Disciples

35 The following day John was again standing with two of his disciples. 36 As Jesus walked by, John looked at him and declared, "Look! There is the Lamb of God!" 37 When John's two disciples heard this, they followed Jesus.

38 Jesus looked around and saw them following. *"What do you want?"* he asked them.

They replied, "Rabbi" (which means "Teacher"), "where are you staying?"

39 *"Come and see,"* he said. It was about four o'clock in the afternoon when they went with him to the place where he was staying, and they remained with him the rest of the day.

40 Andrew, Simon Peter's brother, was one of these men who heard what John said and then followed Jesus. 41 Andrew went to find his brother, Simon, and told him, "We have found the Messiah" (which means "Christ").

42 Then Andrew brought Simon to meet Jesus. Looking intently at Simon, Jesus said, *"Your name is Simon, son of John–but you will be called Cephas"* (which means "Peter").

43 The next day Jesus decided to go to Galilee. He found Philip and said to him, *"Come, follow me."* 44 Philip was from Bethsaida, Andrew and Peter's hometown.

45 Philip went to look for Nathanael and told him, "We have found the very person Moses and the prophets wrote about! His name is Jesus, the son of Joseph from Nazareth."

46 "Nazareth!" exclaimed Nathanael. "Can anything good come from Nazareth?"

"Come and see for yourself," Philip replied.

47 As they approached, Jesus said, *"Now here is a genuine son of Israel–a man of complete integrity."*

48 "How do you know about me?" Nathanael asked.

Jesus replied, *"I could see you under the fig tree before Philip found you."*

49 Then Nathanael exclaimed, "Rabbi, you are the Son of God–the King of Israel!"

50 Jesus asked him, *"Do you believe this just because I told you I had seen you under the fig tree? You will see greater things than this."*

51 Then he said, *"I tell you the truth, you will all see heaven open and the angels of God going up and down on the Son of Man, the one who is the stairway between heaven and earth."*

FYI

Disciple means "learner" and "follower."

Rabbis were spiritual teachers and guides. The Old Testament doesn't mention rabbis. They first appear during the first century A.D.

*Jesus was born in Bethlehem (you can read about that in Matthew 2 and Luke 2), but **Nazareth** was his hometown.*

*Many books in the Old Testament are named after specific prophets, but not all **prophets** had a book named after them.*

Verse 51 mentions things from an Old Testament story when a man named Jacob had a dream and saw angels going up and down a ladder or stairway to heaven.

 Why do you think John includes the names of so many specific towns and villages?

Even without knowing anything about Nazareth, what kind of place do you think it might have been that made people have such a negative opinion of it? Can you think of ways in today's world that people judge others based on where they are from?

What do you think Jesus means when he calls himself "the stairway between heaven and earth"?

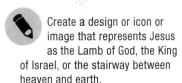 Create a design or icon or image that represents Jesus as the Lamb of God, the King of Israel, or the stairway between heaven and earth.

It's good to be curious about Jesus. It's important to read about what he did and said, to understand more and more about who he really is, to learn from his teaching, to grow closer to him. It's good to intentionally "come and see" more about Jesus every day.

Dear God — Thank you for the invitation to "come and see" more about Jesus. Help me to see him more clearly and truly each day.

CHAPTER 2   The next day there was a wedding celebration in the village of Cana in Galilee. Jesus' mother was there, ₂ and Jesus and his disciples were also invited to the celebration. ₃ The wine supply ran out during the festivities, so Jesus' mother told him, "They have no more wine."

₄ *"Dear woman, that's not our problem,"* Jesus replied. *"My time has not yet come."*

₅ But his mother told the servants, "Do whatever he tells you."

₆ Standing nearby were six stone water jars, used for Jewish ceremonial washing. Each could hold twenty to thirty gallons. ₇ Jesus told the servants, *"Fill the jars with water."* When the jars had been filled, ₈ he said, *"Now dip some out, and take it to the master of ceremonies."* So the servants followed his instructions.

₉ When the master of ceremonies tasted the water that was now wine, not knowing where it had come from (though, of course, the servants knew), he called the bridegroom over. ₁₀ "A host always serves the best wine first," he said. "Then, when everyone has had a lot to drink, he brings out the less expensive wine. But you have kept the best until now!"

₁₁ This miraculous sign at Cana in Galilee was the first time Jesus revealed his glory. And his disciples believed in him.

₁₂ After the wedding he went to Capernaum for a few days with his mother, his brothers, and his disciples.

Jesus Clears the Temple

₁₃ It was nearly time for the Jewish Passover celebration, so Jesus went to Jerusalem. ₁₄ In the Temple area he saw merchants selling cattle, sheep, and doves for sacrifices; he also saw dealers at tables exchanging foreign money. ₁₅ Jesus made a whip from some ropes and chased them all out of the Temple. He drove out the sheep and cattle, scattered the money changers' coins over the floor, and turned over their tables. ₁₆ Then, going over to the people who sold doves, he told them, *"Get these things out of here. Stop turning my Father's house into a marketplace!"*

₁₇ Then his disciples remembered this prophecy from the Scriptures: "Passion for God's house will consume me."

₁₈ But the Jewish leaders demanded, "What are you doing? If God gave you authority to do this, show us a miraculous sign to prove it."

₁₉ *"All right,"* Jesus replied. *"Destroy this temple, and in three days I will raise it up."*

Wedding celebrations in Jesus' time often lasted for several days.

Stone jars filled with water were available for people to wash their hands and dusty feet.

Passover was one of the most important Jewish celebrations. It commemorated a time when God "passed over" every Israelite home that had sacrificial lamb's blood spread on the doorframe. He spared the oldest son from a death plague that struck the Israelites' enemies.

The Temple was in Jerusalem (the capital city) and was the center of Jewish religion. God's presence was believed to be in the center of the Temple in a space called the "holy of holies." People came from all over to offer sacrifices for their sins.

Why do you think Jesus' disciples believed in him after he turned water into wine?

Why do you think Jesus was so angry at the merchants and money exchangers?

What is something in today's world that Jesus might be angry about?

Imagine you were one of the servants who filled the stone jars with water, brought it to the master of ceremonies, and heard his response after tasting it. What would you have thought? How would you have responded? Put that into one sentence or phrase.

Jesus chose the least likely people to have a front-row seat at his first amazing miracle. He didn't choose the powerful. He didn't choose the popular. He didn't choose the up-front, well-known superstar celebrity people. He chose the servants. They were the ones who filled the jars with water. They were the ones who first heard that the water was now wine. They were the ones who witnessed the power of Jesus firsthand. Jesus turns power and prestige upside down.

Dear God — Your miraculous power is amazing. Help me to notice the ways you are at work in the world, even in ordinary circumstances and events.

20 "What!" they exclaimed. "It has taken forty-six years to build this Temple, and you can rebuild it in three days?" 21 But when Jesus said "this temple," he meant his own body. 22 After he was raised from the dead, his disciples remembered he had said this, and they believed both the Scriptures and what Jesus had said.

23 Because of the miraculous signs Jesus did in Jerusalem at the Passover celebration, many began to trust in him. 24 But Jesus didn't trust them, because he knew all about people. 25 No one needed to tell him about human nature, for he knew what was in each person's heart.

Jesus and Nicodemus

CHAPTER 3   There was a man named Nicodemus, a Jewish religious leader who was a Pharisee. 2 After dark one evening, he came to speak with Jesus. "Rabbi," he said, "we all know that God has sent you to teach us. Your miraculous signs are evidence that God is with you."

3 Jesus replied, *"I tell you the truth, unless you are born again, you cannot see the Kingdom of God."*

4 "What do you mean?" exclaimed Nicodemus. "How can an old man go back into his mother's womb and be born again?"

5 Jesus replied, *"I assure you, no one can enter the Kingdom of God without being born of water and the Spirit. 6 Humans can reproduce only human life, but the Holy Spirit gives birth to spiritual life. 7 So don't be surprised when I say, 'You must be born again.' 8 The wind blows wherever it wants. Just as you can hear the wind but can't tell where it comes from or where it is going, so you can't explain how people are born of the Spirit."*

9 "How are these things possible?" Nicodemus asked.

10 Jesus replied, *"You are a respected Jewish teacher, and yet you don't understand these things? 11 I assure you, we tell you what we know and have seen, and yet you won't believe our testimony. 12 But if you don't believe me when I tell you about earthly things, how can you possibly believe if I tell you about heavenly things? 13 No one has ever gone to heaven and returned. But the Son of Man has come down from heaven. 14 And as Moses lifted up the bronze snake on a pole in the wilderness, so the Son of Man must be lifted up, 15 so that everyone who believes in him will have eternal life.*

FYI

*When the New Testament mentions **scriptures**, it refers to the Hebrew scriptures, which is called the Old Testament in Christian Bibles.*

*For more about **Pharisees** see the FYI on page 21.*

*The **Holy Spirit** is part of what Christians call the Trinity — God the Father, God the Son, and God the Holy Spirit. In the Bible the Holy Spirit is sometimes called the Spirit of Christ, sometimes called the Spirit of God, sometimes called just the Spirit, and sometimes called the Holy Spirit.*

*When **Moses** was leading the Israelites through the wilderness, they were once attacked by poisonous snakes. God told Moses, "Make a replica of a poisonous snake and attach it to a pole. All who are bitten will live if they simply look at it!" (Numbers 21:8) Have you noticed that the symbol used by doctors and medical workers features a pole with snakes wrapped around it?*

 Why do you think Nicodemus came to see Jesus at night?

What are some things you don't yet understand about Jesus? About following him?

What are some differences between biological human life and spiritual life?

 Write down one question you'd ask Jesus face-to-face if you had the opportunity.

Being born of God is a mystery. It can't be explained — but it can be experienced. It can't be put into a formula — but it can be felt. It can't be proven in a laboratory — but it can be lived. Everyone who follows Jesus and surrenders their life to him is born again, born of the Spirit, given a new life.

Dear God — Thank you for making it possible to have not just human life but also spiritual life. Please help me grow strong and healthy in my spiritual life.

16 *"For this is how God loved the world: He gave his one and only Son, so that everyone who believes in him will not perish but have eternal life.* 17 *God sent his Son into the world not to judge the world, but to save the world through him.*

18 *"There is no judgment against anyone who believes in him. But anyone who does not believe in him has already been judged for not believing in God's one and only Son.* 19 *And the judgment is based on this fact: God's light came into the world, but people loved the darkness more than the light, for their actions were evil.* 20 *All who do evil hate the light and refuse to go near it for fear their sins will be exposed.* 21 *But those who do what is right come to the light so others can see that they are doing what God wants."*

John the Baptist Exalts Jesus

22 Then Jesus and his disciples left Jerusalem and went into the Judean countryside. Jesus spent some time with them there, baptizing people.

23 At this time John the Baptist was baptizing at Aenon, near Salim, because there was plenty of water there; and people kept coming to him for baptism. 24 (This was before John was thrown into prison.) 25 A debate broke out between John's disciples and a certain Jew over ceremonial cleansing. 26 So John's disciples came to him and said, "Rabbi, the man you met on the other side of the Jordan River, the one you identified as the Messiah, is also baptizing people. And everybody is going to him instead of coming to us."

27 John replied, "No one can receive anything unless God gives it from heaven. 28 You yourselves know how plainly I told you, 'I am not the Messiah. I am only here to prepare the way for him.' 29 It is the bridegroom who marries the bride, and the bridegroom's friend is simply glad to stand with him and hear his vows. Therefore, I am filled with joy at his success. 30 He must become greater and greater, and I must become less and less.

31 "He has come from above and is greater than anyone else. We are of the earth, and we speak of earthly things, but he has come from heaven and is greater than anyone else. 32 He testifies about what he has seen and heard, but how few believe what he tells them! 33 Anyone who accepts his testimony can affirm that God is true. 34 For he is sent by God. He speaks God's words, for God gives him the Spirit without limit.

*You can read the story about **John the Baptist being imprisoned** in Matthew 14:1-12 and Mark 6:14-29. The story must have been so well known that the author of John assumed his readers would know what he was talking about.*

What does it mean that "people love darkness more than light" (verse 19)?

What do you think it means to "believe in Jesus" in verse 16? (Check out verse 36 on the next page for some more insight.)

What do you think John the Baptist meant when he called Jesus "the bridegroom" and himself "the bridegroom's friend" (verse 29)?

Copy verses 16 and 21.

God gave the most precious thing he had — his only son — to show how much he loves people.
Jesus gave the most precious thing he had — his own life — to show how much he loves people.
That's true love: to lay down one's life for others. How will you "lay down your life" for Jesus today and tomorrow and every day of your life?

Dear God — Help me stay away from darkness and live in the light of your truth and love. Help me spread that light to others around me.

35 The Father loves his Son and has put everything into his hands. 36 And anyone who believes in God's Son has eternal life. Anyone who doesn't obey the Son will never experience eternal life but remains under God's angry judgment."

CHAPTER 4 Jesus knew the Pharisees had heard that he was baptizing and making more disciples than John 2 (though Jesus himself didn't baptize them–his disciples did). 3 So he left Judea and returned to Galilee.

4 He had to go through Samaria on the way. 5 Eventually he came to the Samaritan village of Sychar, near the field that Jacob gave to his son Joseph. 6 Jacob's well was there; and Jesus, tired from the long walk, sat wearily beside the well about noontime. 7 Soon a Samaritan woman came to draw water, and Jesus said to her, *"Please give me a drink."* 8 He was alone at the time because his disciples had gone into the village to buy some food.

9 The woman was surprised, for Jews refuse to have anything to do with Samaritans. She said to Jesus, "You are a Jew, and I am a Samaritan woman. Why are you asking me for a drink?"

10 Jesus replied, *"If you only knew the gift God has for you and who you are speaking to, you would ask me, and I would give you living water."*

11 "But sir, you don't have a rope or a bucket," she said, "and this well is very deep. Where would you get this living water? 12 And besides, do you think you're greater than our ancestor Jacob, who gave us this well? How can you offer better water than he and his sons and his animals enjoyed?"

13 Jesus replied, *"Anyone who drinks this water will soon become thirsty again. 14 But those who drink the water I give will never be thirsty again. It becomes a fresh, bubbling spring within them, giving them eternal life."*

15 "Please, sir," the woman said, "give me this water! Then I'll never be thirsty again, and I won't have to come here to get water."

16 *"Go and get your husband,"* Jesus told her.

17 "I don't have a husband," the woman replied.

Jesus said, *"You're right! You don't have a husband– 18 for you have had five husbands, and you aren't even married to the man you're living with now. You certainly spoke the truth!"*

*Long before Jesus was born, the nation of Israel divided into two separate kingdoms. The northern kingdom was called Israel. **Samaria** was its capital. The southern kingdom was called Judah. Jerusalem was its capital city. Eventually both kingdoms were defeated by powerful enemies. The anger and hatred between Jews (or Judeans from what had been the southern kingdom) and Samaritans (from what had been the northern kingdom) ran very deep.*

Jacob *was also called Israel (the story is in Genesis 32). He had 12 sons whose families became the 12 tribes of the nation Israel. His second to youngest son was Joseph. Joseph's brothers sold him into slavery. He eventually ended up in Egypt where he became a powerful leader.*

 What do you think is the connection between "believe" and "obey" (3:36)?

Considering the history between Jews and Samaritans (see more in the FYI at left), what do you learn from this story about how Jesus wants people to treat each other?

What do you think Jesus meant by "living water" that "becomes a fresh, bubbling spring within them"?

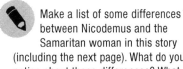 Make a list of some differences between Nicodemus and the Samaritan woman in this story (including the next page). What do you notice about those differences? What is important about those things?

Dry as dust: sometimes life feels that way. It chokes us, wearies us, worries us, and robs us of joy. Jesus offers us living water by offering us himself. He refreshes us, fills us, feeds us, and grows us. We are made from dust, but we don't have to experience a dry and lifeless existence. Instead, we can soak up living water that does more than just refresh us: it gives us real life.

Dear God — Please fill me with your living water, and please help me love others the way Jesus did.

19 "Sir," the woman said, "you must be a prophet. 20 So tell me, why is it that you Jews insist that Jerusalem is the only place of worship, while we Samaritans claim it is here at Mount Gerizim, where our ancestors worshiped?"

21 Jesus replied, *"Believe me, dear woman, the time is coming when it will no longer matter whether you worship the Father on this mountain or in Jerusalem. 22 You Samaritans know very little about the one you worship, while we Jews know all about him, for salvation comes through the Jews. 23 But the time is coming—indeed it's here now—when true worshipers will worship the Father in spirit and in truth. The Father is looking for those who will worship him that way. 24 For God is Spirit, so those who worship him must worship in spirit and in truth."*

25 The woman said, "I know the Messiah is coming—the one who is called Christ. When he comes, he will explain everything to us."

26 Then Jesus told her, *"I am the Messiah!"*

27 Just then his disciples came back. They were shocked to find him talking to a woman, but none of them had the nerve to ask, "What do you want with her?" or "Why are you talking to her?" 28 The woman left her water jar beside the well and ran back to the village, telling everyone, 29 "Come and see a man who told me everything I ever did! Could he possibly be the Messiah?" 30 So the people came streaming from the village to see him.

31 Meanwhile, the disciples were urging Jesus, "Rabbi, eat something."

32 But Jesus replied, *"I have a kind of food you know nothing about."*

33 "Did someone bring him food while we were gone?" the disciples asked each other.

34 Then Jesus explained: *"My nourishment comes from doing the will of God, who sent me, and from finishing his work. 35 You know the saying, 'Four months between planting and harvest.' But I say, wake up and look around. The fields are already ripe for harvest. 36 The harvesters are paid good wages, and the fruit they harvest is people brought to eternal life. What joy awaits both the planter and the harvester alike! 37 You know the saying, 'One plants and another harvests.' And it's true. 38 I sent you to harvest where you didn't plant; others had already done the work, and now you will get to gather the harvest."*

FYI

Jews and **Samaritans** *had their own temples and places of worship.*

Messiah *is the Hebrew word for Anointed One.* **Christ** *is the Greek word for the same thing. The Old Testament prophets often spoke of the coming Messiah who would rescue and restore Israel.*

In the Old Testament, God called himself **"I AM"** *(see Exodus 3:14).*

Rabbi *means teacher.*

What does Jesus' conversation with a Samaritan woman show us about interaction and friendship between different groups of people?

Why do you think the woman was so anxious to tell her village about Jesus?

What do you think it means to worship God "in spirit and in truth"?

List things that planters do.

List things that harvesters do.

How is this like the work of Jesus and his followers?

Deflection is a great skill to have for certain sports, but it's not helpful or good when having an honest conversation with Jesus. In those moments, it's best to be honest, direct, and sincere. Jesus loves to fill broken people who realize it's not where you worship that matters but who you worship. If you are willing to really be with Jesus, you'll have a greater understanding of both who he is (verse 26) and who you are (verse 29).

Dear God — Please teach me how to worship you in spirit and in truth. Help me to always be that kind of worshipper.

39 Many Samaritans from the village believed in Jesus because the woman had said, "He told me everything I ever did!" 40 When they came out to see him, they begged him to stay in their village. So he stayed for two days, 41 long enough for many more to hear his message and believe. 42 Then they said to the woman, "Now we believe, not just because of what you told us, but because we have heard him ourselves. Now we know that he is indeed the Savior of the world."

Jesus Heals an Official's Son

43 At the end of the two days, Jesus went on to Galilee. 44 He himself had said that a prophet is not honored in his own hometown. 45 Yet the Galileans welcomed him, for they had been in Jerusalem at the Passover celebration and had seen everything he did there.

46 As he traveled through Galilee, he came to Cana, where he had turned the water into wine. There was a government official in nearby Capernaum whose son was very sick. 47 When he heard that Jesus had come from Judea to Galilee, he went and begged Jesus to come to Capernaum to heal his son, who was about to die.

48 Jesus asked, *"Will you never believe in me unless you see miraculous signs and wonders?"*

49 The official pleaded, "Lord, please come now before my little boy dies."

50 Then Jesus told him, *"Go back home. Your son will live!"* And the man believed what Jesus said and started home.

51 While the man was on his way, some of his servants met him with the news that his son was alive and well. 52 He asked them when the boy had begun to get better, and they replied, "Yesterday afternoon at one o'clock his fever suddenly disappeared!" 53 Then the father realized that that was the very time Jesus had told him, *"Your son will live."* And he and his entire household believed in Jesus. 54 This was the second miraculous sign Jesus did in Galilee after coming from Judea.

Jesus Heals a Lame Man

CHAPTER 5   Afterward Jesus returned to Jerusalem for one of the Jewish holy days. 2 Inside the city, near the Sheep Gate, was the pool of Bethesda, with five covered porches. 3 Crowds of sick people–blind, lame, or paralyzed–lay on the porches. 5 One of the men lying there had been sick for thirty-eight years. 6 When Jesus saw him and knew he had been ill for a long time, he asked him, *"Would you like to get well?"*

FYI

*Jesus grew up in the region called **Galilee** north of Samaria. See the map on page 14.*

*The **Sheep Gate** is where sheep were brought to the Temple for sacrifice.*

 What are the different reasons people welcomed and believed in Jesus (the Samaritans, the Galileans, the government official)?

Why do you think biblical prophets (or some people today) are often not welcomed or understood in their hometown (or their neighborhood, their school, their family)?

Have you ever felt desperate for Jesus, like the government official did? Why? How did you experience Jesus during that time?

Write here your own statement about why you believe in Jesus. *I believe in Jesus because:*

Sometimes life feels overwhelming, out of control, and desperate. Hope seems far away, even impossible. But with Jesus, there is always hope. Even when he doesn't fix or change things the way we wish, and even when circumstances don't seem to improve, there is still reason to hope because Jesus is always with us, always watching over us, and always loving us.

Dear God — In those times when I sometimes don't sense you near to me, please help me remember who you are and why I believe in you.

7 "I can't, sir," the sick man said, "for I have no one to put me into the pool when the water bubbles up. Someone else always gets there ahead of me."

8 Jesus told him, *"Stand up, pick up your mat, and walk!"*

9 Instantly, the man was healed! He rolled up his sleeping mat and began walking! But this miracle happened on the Sabbath, 10 so the Jewish leaders objected. They said to the man who was cured, "You can't work on the Sabbath! The law doesn't allow you to carry that sleeping mat!"

11 But he replied, "The man who healed me told me, 'Pick up your mat and walk.'"

12 "Who said such a thing as that?" they demanded.

13 The man didn't know, for Jesus had disappeared into the crowd. 14 But afterward Jesus found him in the Temple and told him, *"Now you are well; so stop sinning, or something even worse may happen to you."* 15 Then the man went and told the Jewish leaders that it was Jesus who had healed him.

Jesus Claims to Be God's Son

16 So the Jewish leaders began harassing Jesus for breaking the Sabbath rules. 17 But Jesus replied, *"My Father is always working, and so am I."* 18 So the Jewish leaders tried all the harder to find a way to kill him. For he not only broke the Sabbath, he called God his Father, thereby making himself equal with God.

19 So Jesus explained, *"I tell you the truth, the Son can do nothing by himself. He does only what he sees the Father doing. Whatever the Father does, the Son also does. 20 For the Father loves the Son and shows him everything he is doing. In fact, the Father will show him how to do even greater works than healing this man. Then you will truly be astonished. 21 For just as the Father gives life to those he raises from the dead, so the Son gives life to anyone he wants. 22 In addition, the Father judges no one. Instead, he has given the Son absolute authority to judge, 23 so that everyone will honor the Son, just as they honor the Father. Anyone who does not honor the Son is certainly not honoring the Father who sent him.*

24 *"I tell you the truth, those who listen to my message and believe in God who sent me have eternal life. They will never be condemned for their sins, but they have already passed from death into life.*

25 *"And I assure you that the time is coming, indeed it's here now, when the dead will hear my voice–the voice of the Son of God. And those who listen will live."*

FYI

Have you ever faced an ongoing difficulty or challenge (like the man who'd been sick for 38 years)? What was that like?

Before healing him, why do you think Jesus asked the sick man if he wanted to get well?

Why do you think the religious leaders were so bothered and upset by the things Jesus said and did?

Who would you beg to be with you right now? Samaritan villagers and a government official both begged Jesus to be with them. Jesus is no longer on earth, but you can ask, even beg, for him to be with you right now. In truth, Jesus is already near you because God is present everywhere. Whether you are surrounded by lots of people or none, you are never alone.

Copy verse 24 here.

Dear God — Thank you for sending Jesus to give us a message of truth about you. Help me to listen to it carefully, believe it fully, and follow it joyfully.

37

26 "The Father has life in himself, and he has granted that same life-giving power to his Son. 27 And he has given him authority to judge everyone because he is the Son of Man. 28 Don't be so surprised! Indeed, the time is coming when all the dead in their graves will hear the voice of God's Son, 29 and they will rise again. Those who have done good will rise to experience eternal life, and those who have continued in evil will rise to experience judgment. 30 I can do nothing on my own. I judge as God tells me. Therefore, my judgment is just, because I carry out the will of the one who sent me, not my own will.

Witnesses to Jesus

31 "If I were to testify on my own behalf, my testimony would not be valid. 32 But someone else is also testifying about me, and I assure you that everything he says about me is true. 33 In fact, you sent investigators to listen to John the Baptist, and his testimony about me was true. 34 Of course, I have no need of human witnesses, but I say these things so you might be saved. 35 John was like a burning and shining lamp, and you were excited for a while about his message. 36 But I have a greater witness than John—my teachings and my miracles. The Father gave me these works to accomplish, and they prove that he sent me. 37 And the Father who sent me has testified about me himself. You have never heard his voice or seen him face to face, 38 and you do not have his message in your hearts, because you do not believe me—the one he sent to you.

39 "You search the Scriptures because you think they give you eternal life. But the Scriptures point to me! 40 Yet you refuse to come to me to receive this life.

41 "Your approval means nothing to me, 42 because I know you don't have God's love within you. 43 For I have come to you in my Father's name, and you have rejected me. Yet if others come in their own name, you gladly welcome them. 44 No wonder you can't believe! For you gladly honor each other, but you don't care about the honor that comes from the one who alone is God.

45 "Yet it isn't I who will accuse you before the Father. Moses will accuse you! Yes, Moses, in whom you put your hopes. 46 If you really believed Moses, you would believe me, because he wrote about me. 47 But since you don't believe what he wrote, how will you believe what I say?"

CHAPTER 6   After this, Jesus crossed over to the far side of the Sea of Galilee, also known as the Sea of Tiberias. 2 A huge crowd kept following him wherever he went,

FYI

A **witness** is someone who sees and hears a person's words and actions. If the witness talks about what they've seen and heard, they are **testifying**. We use these same terms today in courtroom settings and other legal contexts.

When Jesus referred to the **scriptures**, he meant what we now call the Old Testament. It was sometimes called "The Law and the Prophets" or "The Law and the Prophets and the Writings." In the original language, the Law was called the Torah, the Prophets were called Nevi'im, and the Writings were called Kethuvim. As a whole, they were known as the Tanakh, using the first letters of each word.

 What do you think Jesus meant when he said the scriptures point to him?

How did Jesus' teaching and miracles witness to his true identity?

How can your words and actions witness to the truth of Jesus?

 List some ways that being a witness to Jesus is similar to being a shining lamp.

We can see the power of God in many things: the majestic night sky, the beauty of nature, the wonder of human life, and the lives of those who love him. We can see the truth of Jesus in many things, most especially in the Bible, all of which points to him. God, Jesus, the Spirit, the scriptures: all these things work together to give us hope, peace, joy, and new life.

Dear God — Thank you for the witness of the Bible and how it reveals the truth about Jesus. Help me to read and understand it so that I can grow closer to you and stronger in my faith.

because they saw his miraculous signs as he healed the sick. ₃ Then Jesus climbed a hill and sat down with his disciples around him. ₄ (It was nearly time for the Jewish Passover celebration.) ₅ Jesus soon saw a huge crowd of people coming to look for him.

Jesus Feeds Thousands

Turning to Philip, he asked, *"Where can we buy bread to feed all these people?"* ₆ He was testing Philip, for he already knew what he was going to do.

₇ Philip replied, "Even if we worked for months, we wouldn't have enough money to feed them!"

₈ Then Andrew, Simon Peter's brother, spoke up. ₉ "There's a young boy here with five barley loaves and two fish. But what good is that with this huge crowd?"

₁₀ *"Tell everyone to sit down,"* Jesus said. So they all sat down on the grassy slopes. (The men alone numbered about 5,000.) ₁₁ Then Jesus took the loaves, gave thanks to God, and distributed them to the people. Afterward he did the same with the fish. And they all ate as much as they wanted. ₁₂ After everyone was full, Jesus told his disciples, *"Now gather the leftovers, so that nothing is wasted."* ₁₃ So they picked up the pieces and filled twelve baskets with scraps left by the people who had eaten from the five barley loaves.

₁₄ When the people saw him do this miraculous sign, they exclaimed, "Surely, he is the Prophet we have been expecting!" ₁₅ When Jesus saw that they were ready to force him to be their king, he slipped away into the hills by himself.

Jesus Walks on Water

₁₆ That evening Jesus' disciples went down to the shore to wait for him. ₁₇ But as darkness fell and Jesus still hadn't come back, they got into the boat and headed across the lake toward Capernaum. ₁₈ Soon a gale swept down upon them, and the sea grew very rough. ₁₉ They had rowed three or four miles when suddenly they saw Jesus walking on the water toward the boat. They were terrified, ₂₀ but he called out to them, *"Don't be afraid. I am here!"* ₂₁ Then they were eager to let him in the boat, and immediately they arrived at their destination!

₂₂ The next day the crowd that had stayed on the far shore saw that the disciples had taken the only boat, and they realized Jesus had not gone with them. ₂₃ Several boats from Tiberias landed near the place where the Lord had blessed the bread and the people had eaten. ₂₄ So when the crowd saw that neither Jesus nor his disciples were there, they got into the boats and went across to Capernaum to look for him.

FYI

Philip, Andrew, and Simon Peter were some of Jesus' disciples.

Simon Peter was also called just Simon, or just Peter, or Cephas.

Barley loaves were common food. In the Old Testament, the prophet Elisha once fed 100 men with 20 small barley loaves and had leftovers (you can read about it in 2 Kings 2:42-44). Many of the Jewish people sitting around Jesus that day would have known the story of Elisha multiplying bread.

 How do you think people responded to Jesus' miracle? How do you think you would have responded?

Why do you think Jesus left by himself when the crowd wanted to force him to be their king?

 Write a prayer thanking God for the food you eat each day.

"Then Jesus took the loaves ... " The miracle took place in the hands of Jesus. The hands that performed so many miracles were the same hands he willingly laid down to be nailed to the cross. Our "not enough" can become a miracle in the hands of Jesus. When we have a need, we should give what we have to Jesus and trust him to do the rest.

Dear God — Help me to remember and believe that no matter what is happening, I don't need to be afraid because you are right here with me.

₂₅ They found him on the other side of the lake and asked, "Rabbi, when did you get here?"

₂₆ Jesus replied, *"I tell you the truth, you want to be with me because I fed you, not because you understood the miraculous signs. ₂₇ But don't be so concerned about perishable things like food. Spend your energy seeking the eternal life that the Son of Man can give you. For God the Father has given me the seal of his approval."*

₂₈ They replied, "We want to perform God's works, too. What should we do?"

₂₉ Jesus told them, *"This is the only work God wants from you: Believe in the one he has sent."*

₃₀ They answered, "Show us a miraculous sign if you want us to believe in you. What can you do? ₃₁ After all, our ancestors ate manna while they journeyed through the wilderness! The Scriptures say, 'Moses gave them bread from heaven to eat.'"

₃₂ Jesus said, *"I tell you the truth, Moses didn't give you bread from heaven. My Father did. And now he offers you the true bread from heaven. ₃₃ The true bread of God is the one who comes down from heaven and gives life to the world."*

₃₄ "Sir," they said, "give us that bread every day."

Jes s, the Bread of Life

₃₅ Jesus replied, *"I am the bread of life. Whoever comes to me will never be hungry again. Whoever believes in me will never be thirsty. ₃₆ But you haven't believed in me even though you have seen me. ₃₇ However, those the Father has given me will come to me, and I will never reject them. ₃₈ For I have come down from heaven to do the will of God who sent me, not to do my own will. ₃₉ And this is the will of God, that I should not lose even one of all those he has given me, but that I should raise them up at the last day. ₄₀ For it is my Father's will that all who see his Son and believe in him should have eternal life. I will raise them up at the last day."*

₄₁ Then the people began to murmur in disagreement because he had said, *"I am the bread that came down from heaven."* ₄₂ They said, "Isn't this Jesus, the son of Joseph? We know his father and mother. How can he say, 'I came down from heaven'?"

₄₃ But Jesus replied, *"Stop complaining about what I said. ₄₄ For no one can come to me unless the Father who sent me draws them to me, and at the last day I will raise them up. ₄₅ As it is written in the Scriptures, 'They will all be taught by God.' Everyone who listens to the Father and learns from him comes to me. ₄₆ (Not that anyone has ever seen the Father; only I, who was sent from God, have seen him.)"*

FYI

Son of Man was a term Jesus sometimes used for himself.

Manna was a special type of bread that God provided each day for the Israelites while they traveled through the wilderness, after he had rescued them from slavery in Egypt. According to the Old Testament story, manna tasted like honey wafers. That story is in Exodus 16.

Joseph was considered to be Jesus' earthly father, though he wasn't his biological father. He was a carpenter. You can read about Joseph in Matthew 1:18-25.

 What are some perishable things (earthly, temporary, not lasting) that many people are concerned about? What perishable things are you personally concerned about?

What do you think Jesus meant when he called himself "bread from heaven" and "true bread of God"?

Copy Jesus' words in verse 29 here.

Jesus called himself the bread of life. In his world, bread was a main portion of people's daily diets. Jesus should be the main portion of our daily life. We need him to feed us, nourish us, and sustain us, each and every day. Bread is very ordinary. But the Bread of Life is the most extraordinary thing ever — because it is Jesus.

Dear God — Thank you for giving me "daily bread" through Jesus and in Jesus. Help me to feast on his truth, love, and goodness every day.

47 "I tell you the truth, anyone who believes has eternal life. 48 Yes, I am the bread of life! 49 Your ancestors ate manna in the wilderness, but they all died. 50 Anyone who eats the bread from heaven, however, will never die. 51 I am the living bread that came down from heaven. Anyone who eats this bread will live forever; and this bread, which I will offer so the world may live, is my flesh."

52 Then the people began arguing with each other about what he meant. "How can this man give us his flesh to eat?" they asked.

53 So Jesus said again, "I tell you the truth, unless you eat the flesh of the Son of Man and drink his blood, you cannot have eternal life within you. 54 But anyone who eats my flesh and drinks my blood has eternal life, and I will raise that person at the last day. 55 For my flesh is true food, and my blood is true drink. 56 Anyone who eats my flesh and drinks my blood remains in me, and I in him. 57 I live because of the living Father who sent me; in the same way, anyone who feeds on me will live because of me. 58 I am the true bread that came down from heaven. Anyone who eats this bread will not die as your ancestors did (even though they ate the manna) but will live forever."

59 He said these things while he was teaching in the synagogue in Capernaum.

60 Many of his disciples said, "This is very hard to understand. How can anyone accept it?"

61 Jesus was aware that his disciples were complaining, so he said to them, "Does this offend you? 62 Then what will you think if you see the Son of Man ascend to heaven again? 63 The Spirit alone gives eternal life. Human effort accomplishes nothing. And the very words I have spoken to you are spirit and life. 64 But some of you do not believe me." (For Jesus knew from the beginning which ones didn't believe, and he knew who would betray him.) 65 Then he said, "That is why I said that people can't come to me unless the Father gives them to me."

66 At this point many of his disciples turned away and deserted him. 67 Then Jesus turned to the Twelve and asked, "Are you also going to leave?"

68 Simon Peter replied, "Lord, to whom would we go? You have the words that give eternal life. 69 We believe, and we know you are the Holy One of God."

70 Then Jesus said, "I chose the twelve of you, but one is a devil." 71 He was speaking of Judas, son of Simon Iscariot, one of the Twelve, who would later betray him.

What do you think Jesus meant when he said, "Anyone who feeds on me will live"? How does a follower of Jesus "feed" on him?

In verse 63 Jesus said, "Human effort accomplishes nothing." But in other places he also said that we are to obey him, to stop sinning, and to love others. How do these different ideas fit together?

Why do you think some people deserted Jesus after his teaching?

Rewrite Peter's response to Jesus (verse 68 and 69) for yourself.

Imagine Jesus looking at you and saying, "Are you also going to leave?" Even the most faithful followers of Jesus can be tempted to "leave" him now and then — to follow their own desires ("just this once") or to choose their own path ("it's really important to me"). We must stay closely connected to Jesus so that we don't leave him in either big or small ways.

Dear God — We believe that Jesus is the bread of life, the Holy One of God, who offers us eternal life. Help us to follow him faithfully and never betray him.

Jesus and His Brothers

CHAPTER 7   After this, Jesus traveled around Galilee. He wanted to stay out of Judea, where the Jewish leaders were plotting his death. 2 But soon it was time for the Jewish Festival of Shelters, 3 and Jesus' brothers said to him, "Leave here and go to Judea, where your followers can see your miracles! 4 You can't become famous if you hide like this! If you can do such wonderful things, show yourself to the world!" 5 For even his brothers didn't believe in him.

6 Jesus replied, *"Now is not the right time for me to go, but you can go anytime. 7 The world can't hate you, but it does hate me because I accuse it of doing evil. 8 You go on. I'm not going to this festival, because my time has not yet come."* 9 After saying these things, Jesus remained in Galilee.

10 But after his brothers left for the festival, Jesus also went, though secretly, staying out of public view. 11 The Jewish leaders tried to find him at the festival and kept asking if anyone had seen him. 12 There was a lot of grumbling about him among the crowds. Some argued, "He's a good man," but others said, "He's nothing but a fraud who deceives the people." 13 But no one had the courage to speak favorably about him in public, for they were afraid of getting in trouble with the Jewish leaders.

Jesus Teaches in the Temple

14 Then, midway through the festival, Jesus went up to the Temple and began to teach. 15 The people were surprised when they heard him. "How does he know so much when he hasn't been trained?" they asked.

16 So Jesus told them, *"My message is not my own; it comes from God who sent me. 17 Anyone who wants to do the will of God will know whether my teaching is from God or is merely my own. 18 Those who speak for themselves want glory only for themselves, but a person who seeks to honor the one who sent him speaks truth, not lies. 19 Moses gave you the law, but none of you obeys it! In fact, you are trying to kill me."*

20 The crowd replied, "You're demon possessed! Who's trying to kill you?"

21 Jesus replied, *"I did one miracle on the Sabbath, and you were amazed. 22 But you work on the Sabbath, too, when you obey Moses' law of circumcision. (Actually, this tradition of circumcision began with the patriarchs, long before the law of Moses.) 23 For if the correct time for circumcising your son falls on the Sabbath, you go ahead and do it so as not to break the law of Moses. So why should you be angry with me for healing a man on the Sabbath? 24 Look beneath the surface so you can judge correctly."*

FYI

Galilee was the northern region of ancient Palestine. Jesus' hometown, Nazareth, was in Galilee. Judea was the southern region of ancient Palestine. Jerusalem was in **Judea**. Samaria was the region between Galilee and Judea. Check out the map on page 14 for more details and locations.

The **Festival of Shelters** (also called Festival of Booths) happened at the end of harvest season. It lasted seven days. Originally it was a time for Israelites to celebrate the ways God provided for his people (see Deuteronomy 16:13-17). In Jesus' day, it also was a reminder of the Exodus journey when the Israelites spent 40 years in the wilderness living in temporary shelters.

Why do you think there was so much tension between Jesus, the crowds, and the religious leaders?

What are some differences between people who "want glory only for themselves" and people who "seek to honor" God (verse 18)?

Jesus implied that it's possible to follow the letter of the law (the exact wording of the instructions) but break the spirit of the law (what it actually means). What are some examples of that in real life?

List some ways that you can seek to honor God (rather than seek glory for yourself) at school, home, work, or with friends.

Jesus' followers wanted fame and glory for him, perhaps because they also wanted it for themselves. It's hard to not care about appearances and recognition in a world that cares about them so much. Jesus found his identity in loving and doing the will of his Father, which brought glory to God. Our identity is found in loving and doing the will of Jesus, which brings glory to him. That's the only fame and glory that matters.

Dear God — Help me become a person who does not seek recognition for myself but instead seeks to honor you in all my words and actions.

*Is Jesus
the Messiah?*

25 Some of the people who lived in Jerusalem started to ask each other, "Isn't this the man they are trying to kill? 26 But here he is, speaking in public, and they say nothing to him. Could our leaders possibly believe that he is the Messiah? 27 But how could he be? For we know where this man comes from. When the Messiah comes, he will simply appear; no one will know where he comes from."

28 While Jesus was teaching in the Temple, he called out, *"Yes, you know me, and you know where I come from. But I'm not here on my own. The one who sent me is true, and you don't know him. 29 But I know him because I come from him, and he sent me to you."* 30 Then the leaders tried to arrest him; but no one laid a hand on him, because his time had not yet come.

31 Many among the crowds at the Temple believed in him. "After all," they said, "would you expect the Messiah to do more miraculous signs than this man has done?"

32 When the Pharisees heard that the crowds were whispering such things, they and the leading priests sent Temple guards to arrest Jesus. 33 But Jesus told them, *"I will be with you only a little longer. Then I will return to the one who sent me. 34 You will search for me but not find me. And you cannot go where I am going."*

35 The Jewish leaders were puzzled by this statement. "Where is he planning to go?" they asked. "Is he thinking of leaving the country and going to the Jews in other lands? Maybe he will even teach the Greeks! 36 What does he mean when he says, 'You will search for me but not find me,' and 'You cannot go where I am going'?"

37 On the last day, the climax of the festival, Jesus stood and shouted to the crowds, *"Anyone who is thirsty may come to me! 38 Anyone who believes in me may come and drink! For the Scriptures declare, 'Rivers of living water will flow from his heart.'"* 39 (When he said "living water," he was speaking of the Spirit, who would be given to everyone believing in him. But the Spirit had not yet been given, because Jesus had not yet entered into his glory.)

40 When the crowds heard him say this, some of them declared, "Surely this man is the Prophet we've been expecting." 41 Others said, "He is the Messiah." Still others said, "But he can't be! Will the Messiah come from Galilee? 42 For the Scriptures clearly state that the Messiah will be born of the royal line of David, in Bethlehem, the village where King David was born." 43 So the crowd was divided about him. 44 Some even wanted him arrested, but no one laid a hand on him.

FYI

*The Jewish people had been waiting for a **Messiah** for generations, someone who would come with God's power to rescue the Jewish nation and rule as their powerful king. Scripture taught that he would be a descendant of King David (see Isaiah 9:7) who would be born in Bethlehem (see Micah 5:2). Jesus was born in Bethlehem but was known as a Nazarene because he grew up and spent his life in Nazareth, a village in Galilee.*

*Jeremiah 2:13 and 7:13 describe God as a fountain of **living water**.*

Why do you think there were such different views and opinions about who Jesus was?

Write some ways that Jesus is like living water.

What do you think Jesus meant by "living water"?

What are some of the different views and opinions people have about Jesus today? How can you know the truth about Jesus, not just people's ideas and opinions?

People couldn't believe that Jesus was the one they were waiting for because he didn't fit their expectations. Jesus responded with kindness and truth. He was sent by God. Jesus' honest responses made some people want to follow him, and made others mad enough to kill him. What's your response to Jesus telling the truth about who he is?

Dear God — Help me to learn the truth about you so that I'm not swayed by false ideas or influenced by mistaken opinions.

45 When the Temple guards returned without having arrested Jesus, the leading priests and Pharisees demanded, "Why didn't you bring him in?"

46 "We have never heard anyone speak like this!" the guards responded.

47 "Have you been led astray, too?" the Pharisees mocked. 48 "Is there a single one of us rulers or Pharisees who believes in him? 49 This foolish crowd follows him, but they are ignorant of the law. God's curse is on them!"

50 Then Nicodemus, the leader who had met with Jesus earlier, spoke up. 51 "Is it legal to convict a man before he is given a hearing?" he asked.

52 They replied, "Are you from Galilee, too? Search the Scriptures and see for yourself—no prophet ever comes from Galilee!"

[The most ancient Greek manuscripts do not include John 7:53-8:11.]

53 Then the meeting broke up, and everybody went home.

A Woman Caught in Adultery

CHAPTER 8   Jesus returned to the Mount of Olives, 2 but early the next morning he was back again at the Temple. A crowd soon gathered, and he sat down and taught them. 3 As he was speaking, the teachers of religious law and the Pharisees brought a woman who had been caught in the act of adultery. They put her in front of the crowd.

4 "Teacher," they said to Jesus, "this woman was caught in the act of adultery. 5 The law of Moses says to stone her. What do you say?"

6 They were trying to trap him into saying something they could use against him, but Jesus stooped down and wrote in the dust with his finger. 7 They kept demanding an answer, so he stood up again and said, *"All right, but let the one who has never sinned throw the first stone!"* 8 Then he stooped down again and wrote in the dust.

9 When the accusers heard this, they slipped away one by one, beginning with the oldest, until only Jesus was left in the middle of the crowd with the woman. 10 Then Jesus stood up again and said to the woman, *"Where are your accusers? Didn't even one of them condemn you?"*

11 "No, Lord," she said.

And Jesus said, *"Neither do I. Go and sin no more."*

. . . .

Jesus is the Light of the World

12 Jesus spoke to the people once more and said, *"I am the light of the world. If you follow me, you won't have to walk in darkness, because you will have the light that leads to life."*

*The story of **Nicodemus** meeting with Jesus is in John 3.*

*The **Mount of Olives** is just outside of Jerusalem.*

The story in 7:53-8:11 is not in the very earliest manuscripts of the New Testament. Most scholars believe that it is a truthful representation of Jesus that shows his patience, compassion, forgiveness, and call to obedience. It may have been that this story was told orally for many generations before being written down and included in John. No one is absolutely sure about the exact details, which is why Bibles include the background note that you see between 7:52 and 7:53.

What are your thoughts about Nicodemus based on his earlier conversation with Jesus (in chapter 3) and his words here in 7:51?

Why do you think Jesus bent down to write in the dirt when the religious leaders asked him a question?

Why do you think Jesus both forgave the woman (did not condemn her) and also told her to "go and sin no more"?

Copy verse 12 here. Think about how Jesus is like light. Think about how life is sometimes like walking in darkness.

The religious leaders mocked the Temple guards for listening to and admiring Jesus' teaching. They mocked the crowds for following him, even calling them fools. It is a wise person who listens to Jesus, learns from Jesus, and follows Jesus, even if the world calls that person a fool. Being a "fool for Jesus" is the wisest thing anyone can do.

Dear God — Thank you for being compassionate and forgiving. Help me to follow you and live in your light so that I don't walk in darkness and face temptation to sin.

13 The Pharisees replied, "You are making those claims about yourself! Such testimony is not valid."

14 Jesus told them, *"These claims are valid even though I make them about myself. For I know where I came from and where I am going, but you don't know this about me. 15 You judge me by human standards, but I do not judge anyone. 16 And if I did, my judgment would be correct in every respect because I am not alone. The Father who sent me is with me. 17 Your own law says that if two people agree about something, their witness is accepted as fact. 18 I am one witness, and my Father who sent me is the other."*

19 "Where is your father?" they asked.

Jesus answered, *"Since you don't know who I am, you don't know who my Father is. If you knew me, you would also know my Father."* 20 Jesus made these statements while he was teaching in the section of the Temple known as the Treasury. But he was not arrested, because his time had not yet come.

*Jesus Warns
Unbelievers*
21 Later Jesus said to them again, *"I am going away. You will search for me but will die in your sin. You cannot come where I am going."*

22 The people asked, "Is he planning to commit suicide? What does he mean, 'You cannot come where I am going'?"

23 Jesus continued, *"You are from below; I am from above. You belong to this world; I do not. 24 That is why I said that you will die in your sins; for unless you believe that I am who I claim to be, you will die in your sins."*

25 "Who are you?" they demanded.

Jesus replied, *"The one I have always claimed to be. 26 I have much to say about you and much to condemn, but I won't. For I say only what I have heard from the one who sent me, and he is completely truthful."* 27 But they still didn't understand that he was talking about his Father.

28 So Jesus said, *"When you have lifted up the Son of Man on the cross, then you will understand that I am he. I do nothing on my own but say only what the Father taught me. 29 And the one who sent me is with me–he has not deserted me. For I always do what pleases him."* 30 Then many who heard him say these things believed in him.

31Jesus said to the people who believed in him, *"You are truly my disciples if you remain faithful to my teachings. 32 And you will know the truth, and the truth will set you free."*

FYI

Deuteronomy 19:15 says, "You must not convict anyone of a crime on the testimony of only one witness. The facts of the case must be established by the testimony of **two or three witnesses**."

Below and **above** don't refer to actual locations. They indicate the difference between earthly and heavenly realities.

? What do you think Jesus meant when he said, "If you knew me, you would also know my Father"?

Why do you think many people believed in Jesus in this moment (verse 30)?

What do you think Jesus meant when he said "the truth will set you free"? How does truth free us? What does it free us from?

Use verse 31 to write a short description of a disciple, which includes everyone who gives their life to Jesus and lives for him.

The world is filled with messages that are lies, or half-truths at best. Lies about what really matters. Lies about how life works. Lies about meaning and purpose. Lies about money. Lies about pleasure. Lies about success. Lies about other people. Jesus is the source of truth. When we know the truth about God, about life, about humanity, and about love, we can be truly free to live and be who God created us to be.

Dear God — Thank you for the words of Jesus. Help me to understand them and to be set free by the truth he teaches.

33 "But we are descendants of Abraham," they said. "We have never been slaves to anyone. What do you mean, 'You will be set free'?"

34 Jesus replied, *"I tell you the truth, everyone who sins is a slave of sin. 35 A slave is not a permanent member of the family, but a son is part of the family forever. 36 So if the Son sets you free, you are truly free. 37 Yes, I realize that you are descendants of Abraham. And yet some of you are trying to kill me because there's no room in your hearts for my message. 38 I am telling you what I saw when I was with my Father. But you are following the advice of your father."*

39 "Our father is Abraham!" they declared.

"No," Jesus replied, *"for if you were really the children of Abraham, you would follow his example. 40 Instead, you are trying to kill me because I told you the truth, which I heard from God. Abraham never did such a thing. 41 No, you are imitating your real father."*

They replied, "We aren't illegitimate children! God himself is our true Father."

42 Jesus told them, *"If God were your Father, you would love me, because I have come to you from God. I am not here on my own, but he sent me. 43 Why can't you understand what I am saying? It's because you can't even hear me! 44 For you are the children of your father the devil, and you love to do the evil things he does. He was a murderer from the beginning. He has always hated the truth, because there is no truth in him. When he lies, it is consistent with his character; for he is a liar and the father of lies. 45 So when I tell the truth, you just naturally don't believe me! 46 Which of you can truthfully accuse me of sin? And since I am telling you the truth, why don't you believe me? 47 Anyone who belongs to God listens gladly to the words of God. But you don't listen because you don't belong to God."*

48 The people retorted, "You Samaritan devil! Didn't we say all along that you were possessed by a demon?"

49 *"No,"* Jesus said, *"I have no demon in me. For I honor my Father—and you dishonor me. 50 And though I have no wish to glorify myself, God is going to glorify me. He is the true judge. 51 I tell you the truth, anyone who obeys my teaching will never die!"*

52 The people said, "Now we know you are possessed by a demon. Even Abraham and the prophets died, but you say, 'Anyone who obeys my teaching will never die.'

FYI

Abraham's story is told in Genesis 12-25. (You can read about it in The Big Story on pages 12 and 13.) God made a covenant with Abraham: "This is the everlasting covenant: I will always be your God and the God of your descendants after you" (Genesis 17:7).

Slavery was widespread in the ancient world and accepted in most cultures, but the Bible speaks strongly against it in places like 1 Timothy 1:10 (where slave-traders are included in a list of lawless people) and Revelation 18:13 (which condemns slavery and other things).

The word for **devil** in verse 44 means someone who slanders or accuses falsely.

What do you think Jesus meant when he said "everyone who sins is a slave of sin"?

What do these verses say about truth and lies?

What are some of the biggest lies people believe about God? about Jesus? about people?

Think about things that make God our true, good, and loving Father. Write them here.

Jesus' opponents didn't like the things he said. Because they didn't like the message, they attacked the messenger. People often do that — try to make someone look bad so they don't have to listen to them. But Jesus calls his opponents out — "If I am telling the truth, why don't you believe me?" People may try to avoid the teachings of Jesus, but truth will win in the end.

Dear God — Please help me make room in my heart for your message of truth. Please protect me from the lies of the world.

53 "Are you greater than our father Abraham? He died, and so did the prophets. Who do you think you are?"

54 Jesus answered, *"If I want glory for myself, it doesn't count. But it is my Father who will glorify me. You say, 'He is our God,'* 55 *but you don't even know him. I know him. If I said otherwise, I would be as great a liar as you! But I do know him and obey him.* 56 *Your father Abraham rejoiced as he looked forward to my coming. He saw it and was glad."*

57 The people said, "You aren't even fifty years old. How can you say you have seen Abraham?"

58 Jesus answered, *"I tell you the truth, before Abraham was even born, I am!"* 59 At that point they picked up stones to throw at him. But Jesus was hidden from them and left the Temple.

Jesus Heals a Man Born Blind

CHAPTER 9   As Jesus was walking along, he saw a man who had been blind from birth. 2 "Rabbi," his disciples asked him, "why was this man born blind? Was it because of his own sins or his parents' sins?"

3 "It was not because of his sins or his parents' sins," Jesus answered. *"This happened so the power of God could be seen in him.* 4 *We must quickly carry out the tasks assigned us by the one who sent us. The night is coming, and then no one can work.* 5 *But while I am here in the world, I am the light of the world."*

6 Then he spit on the ground, made mud with the saliva, and spread the mud over the blind man's eyes. 7 He told him, *"Go wash yourself in the pool of Siloam"* (Siloam means "sent"). So the man went and washed and came back seeing!

8 His neighbors and others who knew him as a blind beggar asked each other, "Isn't this the man who used to sit and beg?" 9 Some said he was, and others said, "No, he just looks like him!"

But the beggar kept saying, "Yes, I am the same one!"

10 They asked, "Who healed you? What happened?"

11 He told them, "The man they call Jesus made mud and spread it over my eyes and told me, 'Go to the pool of Siloam and wash yourself.' So I went and washed, and now I can see!"

12 "Where is he now?" they asked.

FYI

I AM was one way God referred to himself in the Old Testament.

*Jesus used **saliva** in three different healing stories: here in John 9, in Mark 7:33, and in Mark 8:23. Some people think he did this because an ancient Jewish tradition claimed that the saliva of a legitimate first-born son had healing properties. Some people think Jesus mixed mud and saliva in this story because making bricks (clay combined with water) was forbidden on the Sabbath (see 9:15 on the next page). Still others believe that Jesus' command to wash off mud with water was a symbol of washing off sins and being cleansed by Jesus' death and resurrection.*

 What do you think it was like for people to hear Jesus say he was God's son and was sent by God?

 Think about how Jesus has worked in your life, revealing thoughts that you should change, revealing an attitude that doesn't honor him, or something else. If someone were to ask you what happened (like in verse 10), what would you say?

What do you notice in verses 6-7 and then in verse 11? What seems important about that?

Jesus washes. The blind man sees. What an odd combination. Dirty and clean go together. Blind and see go together. But wash and see? It seems like a mismatch. But in terms of hearts and souls, they go together perfectly. Humanity is stained with sin because it refuses to see the truth of Jesus. When Jesus washes hearts, he also opens the eyes of human souls so they can finally see him for who he really is: God in flesh.

Dear God — Thank you for noticing everyone and for caring about their lives and circumstances. Help me to love others like that.

57

"I don't know," he replied.

13 Then they took the man who had been blind to the Pharisees, 14 because it was on the Sabbath that Jesus had made the mud and healed him. 15 The Pharisees asked the man all about it. So he told them, "He put the mud over my eyes, and when I washed it away, I could see!"

16 Some of the Pharisees said, "This man Jesus is not from God, for he is working on the Sabbath." Others said, "But how could an ordinary sinner do such miraculous signs?" So there was a deep division of opinion among them.

17 Then the Pharisees again questioned the man who had been blind and demanded, "What's your opinion about this man who healed you?"

The man replied, "I think he must be a prophet."

18 The Jewish leaders still refused to believe the man had been blind and could now see, so they called in his parents. 19 They asked them, "Is this your son? Was he born blind? If so, how can he now see?"

20 His parents replied, "We know this is our son and that he was born blind, 21 but we don't know how he can see or who healed him. Ask him. He is old enough to speak for himself." 22 His parents said this because they were afraid of the Jewish leaders, who had announced that anyone saying Jesus was the Messiah would be expelled from the synagogue. 23 That's why they said, "He is old enough. Ask him."

24 So for the second time they called in the man who had been blind and told him, "God should get the glory for this, because we know this man Jesus is a sinner."

25 "I don't know whether he is a sinner," the man replied. "But I know this: I was blind, and now I can see!"

26 "But what did he do?" they asked. "How did he heal you?"

27 "Look!" the man exclaimed. "I told you once. Didn't you listen? Why do you want to hear it again? Do you want to become his disciples, too?"

28 Then they cursed him and said, "You are his disciple, but we are disciples of Moses! 29 We know God spoke to Moses, but we don't even know where this man comes from."

30 "Why, that's very strange!" the man replied. "He healed my eyes, and yet you don't know where he comes from? 31 We know that God doesn't listen to sinners, but he is ready to hear those who worship him and do his will. 32 Ever since the world began,

FYI

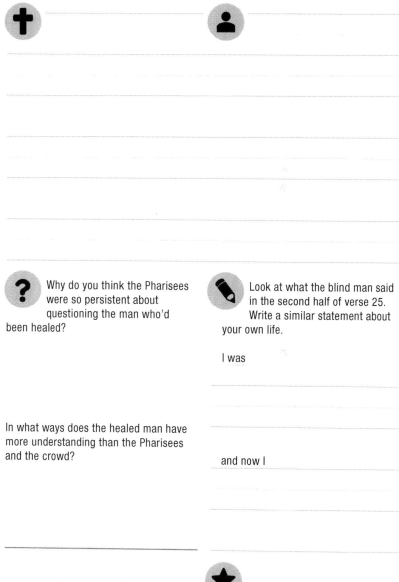

? Why do you think the Pharisees were so persistent about questioning the man who'd been healed?

In what ways does the healed man have more understanding than the Pharisees and the crowd?

Look at what the blind man said in the second half of verse 25. Write a similar statement about your own life.

I was

and now I

Over and over, the leaders saw and heard evidence of Jesus' miraculous power. Over and over, they refused to believe. Over and over, they rejected what was so obviously true. People refuse and reject Jesus on a daily basis, determinedly clinging to their own sense of superiority. God allows us the freedom to stubbornly refuse and reject him — but it breaks his heart.

Dear God — Thank you for helping your followers see Jesus, see you, and see truth. Help me to see those things clearly.

no one has been able to open the eyes of someone born blind. 33 If this man were not from God, he couldn't have done it."

34 "You were born a total sinner!" they answered. "Are you trying to teach us?" And they threw him out of the synagogue.

35 When Jesus heard what had happened, he found the man and asked, *"Do you believe in the Son of Man?"*

36 The man answered, "Who is he, sir? I want to believe in him."

37 *"You have seen him,"* Jesus said, *"and he is speaking to you!"*

38 "Yes, Lord, I believe!" the man said. And he worshiped Jesus.

39 Then Jesus told him, *"I entered this world to render judgment—to give sight to the blind and to show those who think they see that they are blind."*

40 Some Pharisees who were standing nearby heard him and asked, "Are you saying we're blind?"

41 *"If you were blind, you wouldn't be guilty,"* Jesus replied. *"But you remain guilty because you claim you can see.*

Jesus is the Good Shepherd **CHAPTER 10** *"I tell you the truth, anyone who sneaks over the wall of a sheepfold, rather than going through the gate, must surely be a thief and a robber! 2 But the one who enters through the gate is the shepherd of the sheep. 3 The gatekeeper opens the gate for him, and the sheep recognize his voice and come to him. He calls his own sheep by name and leads them out. 4 After he has gathered his own flock, he walks ahead of them, and they follow him because they know his voice. 5 They won't follow a stranger; they will run from him because they don't know his voice."*

6 Those who heard Jesus use this illustration didn't understand what he meant, 7 so he explained it to them: *"I tell you the truth, I am the gate for the sheep. 8 All who came before me were thieves and robbers. But the true sheep did not listen to them. 9 Yes, I am the gate. Those who come in through me will be saved. They will come and go freely and will find good pastures. 10 The thief's purpose is to steal and kill and destroy. My purpose is to give them a rich and satisfying life.*

11 *"I am the good shepherd. The good shepherd sacrifices his life for the sheep. 12 A hired hand will run when he sees a wolf coming. He will abandon the sheep because they don't belong to him and he isn't their shepherd. And so the wolf attacks them and*

Synagogues *were places of worship in the towns and villages. The Temple — the center of Jewish religion — was in Jerusalem.*

Son of Man *is a title Jesus sometimes used for himself. It's used many times in the Old Testament. In the book of Daniel (7:13-14) it refers to a future ruler from heaven who reigns over all the world and whose Kingdom never ends.*

What ideas in today's world "steal and kill and destroy" the life God intends for us?

In what ways does Jesus give us "rich and satisfying life" (rich doesn't refer to money, and satisfying doesn't mean successful)?

Why do you think Jesus used so many images and metaphors to teach people?

List some differences between Jesus, our true shepherd, and all the false, lying, untrue "gods" people sometimes follow.

Jesus is like a shepherd. He cares for us, protects us, feeds us, watches over us, looks for us when we wander away, and knows each of us. We are like sheep — in need of a guide, protector, caretaker, and rescuer. Best of all, Jesus is a GOOD shepherd. All he says and does is good. Jesus is our good shepherd. Jesus is your good shepherd. Follow him closely and carefully. (Check out Psalm 23 for more about God as our shepherd.)

Dear God — Thank you for being our good shepherd who both guards us and guides us.

scatters the flock. 13 The hired hand runs away because he's working only for the money and doesn't really care about the sheep.

14 *"I am the good shepherd; I know my own sheep, and they know me, 15 just as my Father knows me and I know the Father. So I sacrifice my life for the sheep. 16 I have other sheep, too, that are not in this sheepfold. I must bring them also. They will listen to my voice, and there will be one flock with one shepherd.*

17 *"The Father loves me because I sacrifice my life so I may take it back again. 18 No one can take my life from me. I sacrifice it voluntarily. For I have the authority to lay it down when I want to and also to take it up again. For this is what my Father has commanded."*

19 When he said these things, the people were again divided in their opinions about him. 20 Some said, "He's demon possessed and out of his mind. Why listen to a man like that?" 21 Others said, "This doesn't sound like a man possessed by a demon! Can a demon open the eyes of the blind?"

Jesus Claims to be God's Son

22 It was now winter, and Jesus was in Jerusalem at the time of Hanukkah, the Festival of Dedication. 23 He was in the Temple, walking through the section known as Solomon's Colonnade. 24 The people surrounded him and asked, "How long are you going to keep us in suspense? If you are the Messiah, tell us plainly."

25 Jesus replied, *"I have already told you, and you don't believe me. The proof is the work I do in my Father's name. 26 But you don't believe me because you are not my sheep. 27 My sheep listen to my voice; I know them, and they follow me. 28 I give them eternal life, and they will never perish. No one can snatch them away from me, 29 for my Father has given them to me, and he is more powerful than anyone else. No one can snatch them from the Father's hand. 30 The Father and I are one."*

31 Once again the people picked up stones to kill him. 32 Jesus said, *"At my Father's direction I have done many good works. For which one are you going to stone me?"*

33 They replied, "We're stoning you not for any good work, but for blasphemy! You, a mere man, claim to be God."

34 Jesus replied, *"It is written in your own Scriptures that God said to certain leaders of the people, 'I say, you are gods!' 35 And you know that the Scriptures cannot*

FYI

 Why do you think people had such different views about Jesus?

 List some of the ways that you listen to Jesus' voice and follow him (verse 27).

How is the relationship between Jesus and his Father similar to the relationship between Jesus and his followers (verses 14 and 15)?

It's hard to imagine that anyone would willingly give up their life to save another. Jesus is the source of life and creator of humanity. Of all people, he has the most right to not give up his life for even one person, let alone all people. But Jesus does unexpected and shocking things all the time, including sacrificing his life voluntarily for people who would never sacrifice their own life for anyone.

Dear God — Thank you for sacrificing to save us. Thank you for speaking to us and knowing us. Help us to listen to your voice and follow you faithfully.

63

be altered. So if those people who received God's message were called 'gods,' 36 why do you call it blasphemy when I say, 'I am the Son of God'? After all, the Father set me apart and sent me into the world. 37 Don't believe me unless I carry out my Father's work. 38 But if I do his work, believe in the evidence of the miraculous works I have done, even if you don't believe me. Then you will know and understand that the Father is in me, and I am in the Father."

39 Once again they tried to arrest him, but he got away and left them. 40 He went beyond the Jordan River near the place where John was first baptizing and stayed there awhile. 41 And many followed him. "John didn't perform miraculous signs," they remarked to one another, "but everything he said about this man has come true." 42 And many who were there believed in Jesus.

Jesus Raises Lazarus

CHAPTER 11   A man named Lazarus was sick. He lived in Bethany with his sisters, Mary and Martha. 2 This is the Mary who later poured the expensive perfume on the Lord's feet and wiped them with her hair. Her brother, Lazarus, was sick. 3 So the two sisters sent a message to Jesus telling him, "Lord, your dear friend is very sick."

4 But when Jesus heard about it he said, *"Lazarus's sickness will not end in death. No, it happened for the glory of God so that the Son of God will receive glory from this."* 5 So although Jesus loved Martha, Mary, and Lazarus, 6 he stayed where he was for the next two days. 7 Finally, he said to his disciples, *"Let's go back to Judea."*

8 But his disciples objected. "Rabbi," they said, "only a few days ago the people in Judea were trying to stone you. Are you going there again?"

9 Jesus replied, *"There are twelve hours of daylight every day. During the day people can walk safely. They can see because they have the light of this world. 10 But at night there is danger of stumbling because they have no light."* 11 Then he said, *"Our friend Lazarus has fallen asleep, but now I will go and wake him up."*

12 The disciples said, "Lord, if he is sleeping, he will soon get better!" 13 They thought Jesus meant Lazarus was simply sleeping, but Jesus meant Lazarus had died.

14 So he told them plainly, *"Lazarus is dead. 15 And for your sakes, I'm glad I wasn't there, for now you will really believe. Come, let's go see him."*

16 Thomas, nicknamed the Twin, said to his fellow disciples, "Let's go, too–and die with Jesus."

FYI

*You can read another story about **Mary and Martha** in Luke 10:38-42.*

***Bethany** was in Judea, very near to Jerusalem, on the west side of the Jordan River. Jesus had gone to the east side of the river just before this to get away from people who were trying to arrest him.*

*In the ancient world, people sometimes talked about death symbolically as **falling asleep**. Even today the common phrase "rest in peace" connects death to the image of sleep.*

 What do you think the disciples thought about Jesus' delayed response to Mary and Martha?

What do you think Jesus meant when he talked about daylight/light of the world and stumbling because of no light?

If you'd been with Jesus, would you have responded like Thomas did (verse 16) or would you have wanted to stay away from danger? Why?

 Think about someone you know who needs the comfort and love of Jesus. Tell God about that now, like Mary and Martha did in this story.

Jesus' plans and actions don't always make sense to us. He loved Lazarus, but didn't rush to heal him. He loves us, but doesn't always respond in the way we hope or expect. We can trust Jesus' plans, timing, and actions because he is good, loving, true, and faithful.

Dear God — Thank you that when we need you and when our family and friends need you, we can tell you about it, knowing you will listen.

17 When Jesus arrived at Bethany, he was told that Lazarus had already been in his grave for four days. 18 Bethany was only a few miles down the road from Jerusalem, 19 and many of the people had come to console Martha and Mary in their loss. 20 When Martha got word that Jesus was coming, she went to meet him. But Mary stayed in the house. 21 Martha said to Jesus, "Lord, if only you had been here, my brother would not have died. 22 But even now I know that God will give you whatever you ask."

23 Jesus told her, *"Your brother will rise again."*

24 "Yes," Martha said, "he will rise when everyone else rises, at the last day."

25 Jesus told her, *"I am the resurrection and the life. Anyone who believes in me will live, even after dying. 26 Everyone who lives in me and believes in me will never ever die. Do you believe this, Martha?"*

27 "Yes, Lord," she told him. "I have always believed you are the Messiah, the Son of God, the one who has come into the world from God." 28 Then she returned to Mary. She called Mary aside from the mourners and told her, "The Teacher is here and wants to see you." 29 So Mary immediately went to him.

30 Jesus had stayed outside the village, at the place where Martha met him. 31 When the people who were at the house consoling Mary saw her leave so hastily, they assumed she was going to Lazarus's grave to weep. So they followed her there. 32 When Mary arrived and saw Jesus, she fell at his feet and said, "Lord, if only you had been here, my brother would not have died."

33 When Jesus saw her weeping and saw the other people wailing with her, a deep anger welled up within him, and he was deeply troubled. 34 *"Where have you put him?"* he asked them.

They told him, "Lord, come and see." 35 Then Jesus wept. 36 The people who were standing nearby said, "See how much he loved him!" 37 But some said, "This man healed a blind man. Couldn't he have kept Lazarus from dying?"

38 Jesus was still angry as he arrived at the tomb, a cave with a stone rolled across its entrance. 39 *"Roll the stone aside,"* Jesus told them.

But Martha, the dead man's sister, protested, "Lord, he has been dead for four days. The smell will be terrible."

40 Jesus responded, *"Didn't I tell you that you would see God's glory if you believe?"* 41 So they rolled the stone aside. Then Jesus looked up to heaven and said,

FYI

In Jesus' time, when people died their bodies were anointed with perfume and wrapped in burial cloths. Usually on the same day, the body was placed in a burial cave that was sealed shut with a stone. The time of mourning sometimes lasted 30 days. After a year, the tomb would be opened and the bones of the dead person would be gathered together into a box — almost like a small coffin — and that box would be stored in the back of the burial cave with ancestors and other deceased family members.

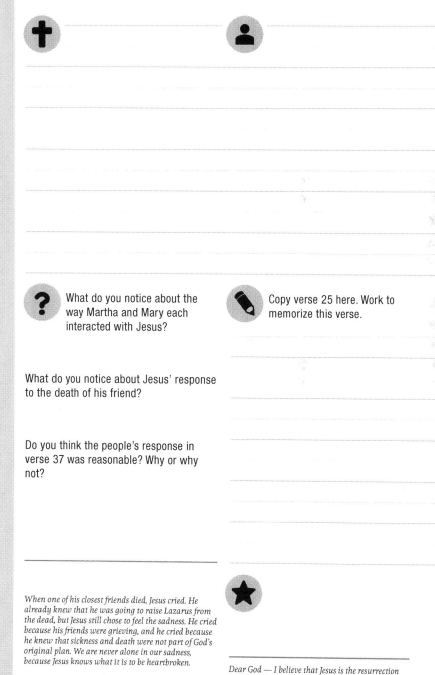

What do you notice about the way Martha and Mary each interacted with Jesus?

Copy verse 25 here. Work to memorize this verse.

What do you notice about Jesus' response to the death of his friend?

Do you think the people's response in verse 37 was reasonable? Why or why not?

When one of his closest friends died, Jesus cried. He already knew that he was going to raise Lazarus from the dead, but Jesus still chose to feel the sadness. He cried because his friends were grieving, and he cried because he knew that sickness and death were not part of God's original plan. We are never alone in our sadness, because Jesus knows what it is to be heartbroken.

Dear God — I believe that Jesus is the resurrection and the life. I believe that through him, real life is possible both now and forever.

67

"Father, thank you for hearing me. 42 You always hear me, but I said it out loud for the sake of all these people standing here, so that they will believe you sent me." 43 Then Jesus shouted, *"Lazarus, come out!"* 44 And the dead man came out, his hands and feet bound in graveclothes, his face wrapped in a headcloth. Jesus told them, *"Unwrap him and let him go!"*

45 Many of the people who were with Mary believed in Jesus when they saw this happen. 46 But some went to the Pharisees and told them what Jesus had done. 47 Then the leading priests and Pharisees called the high council together. "What are we going to do?" they asked each other. "This man certainly performs many miraculous signs. 48 If we allow him to go on like this, soon everyone will believe in him. Then the Roman army will come and destroy both our Temple and our nation."

49 Caiaphas, who was high priest at that time, said, "You don't know what you're talking about! 50 You don't realize that it's better for you that one man should die for the people than for the whole nation to be destroyed."

51 He did not say this on his own; as high priest at that time he was led to prophesy that Jesus would die for the entire nation. 52 And not only for that nation, but to bring together and unite all the children of God scattered around the world.

53 So from that time on, the Jewish leaders began to plot Jesus' death. 54 As a result, Jesus stopped his public ministry among the people and left Jerusalem. He went to a place near the wilderness, to the village of Ephraim, and stayed there with his disciples.

55 It was now almost time for the Jewish Passover celebration, and many people from all over the country arrived in Jerusalem several days early so they could go through the purification ceremony before Passover began. 56 They kept looking for Jesus, but as they stood around in the Temple, they said to each other, "What do you think? He won't come for Passover, will he?" 57 Meanwhile, the leading priests and Pharisees had publicly ordered that anyone seeing Jesus must report it immediately so they could arrest him.

Jesus Anointed with Perfume

CHAPTER 12 Six days before the Passover celebration began, Jesus arrived in Bethany, the home of Lazarus–the man he had raised from the dead. 2 A dinner was prepared in Jesus' honor. Martha served, and Lazarus was among those who ate with

FYI

The **high council**, known as the Sanhedrin, had first been established about 200 years before Jesus lived. It included high priests, tribal elders, and legal scribes. The Sanhedrin included people from the two different religious groups: the Pharisees (who are mentioned throughout the book of John) and the Sadducees (who are mentioned in Matthew, Mark, Luke, and Acts). The Sadducees were the majority party. They did not believe in the resurrection of the body, the immortality of the soul, or spirits and angels.

The **high priest** presided over the Sanhedrin. Once a year, the high priest entered the most sacred part of the Temple, the Holy of Holies, and offered a sacrifice on the Day of Atonement. In the book of Hebrews, Jesus is called our great high priest. At his death, the curtain to the Holy of Holies was torn in two.

Devout Jews traveled to Jerusalem each year for the **Passover celebration.**

 Why do you think many of the people with Mary responded differently to Jesus' miracle than the religious leaders did (verses 45-48, 53)?

 The tension and intrigue were very high during this time. Spend some time thinking about the situation and what it must have been like for the people in Jerusalem, for Jesus' followers, and for Jesus himself.

"Unwrap him." While Jesus certainly did the heavy lifting in raising Lazarus from the dead, he didn't stop with just bringing him back to life. He invited the community of grieving people to help Lazarus take off his grave clothes. It is a gift that Jesus invites us to participate with him. It is a gift that we are part of a larger community, the family of God.

Dear God — Thank you for the resurrection power of Jesus, who both raised Lazarus from the dead and who brings us from death to life when we follow him as Lord.

him. 3 Then Mary took a twelve-ounce jar of expensive perfume made from essence of nard, and she anointed Jesus' feet with it, wiping his feet with her hair. The house was filled with the fragrance.

4 But Judas Iscariot, the disciple who would soon betray him, said, 5 "That perfume was worth a year's wages. It should have been sold and the money given to the poor." 6 Not that he cared for the poor—he was a thief, and since he was in charge of the disciples' money, he often stole some for himself.

7 Jesus replied, *"Leave her alone. She did this in preparation for my burial. 8 You will always have the poor among you, but you will not always have me."*

9 When all the people heard of Jesus' arrival, they flocked to see him and also to see Lazarus, the man Jesus had raised from the dead. 10 Then the leading priests decided to kill Lazarus, too, 11 for it was because of him that many of the people had deserted them and believed in Jesus.

Jesus Enters Jerusalem

12 The next day, the news that Jesus was on the way to Jerusalem swept through the city. A large crowd of Passover visitors 13 took palm branches and went down the road to meet him. They shouted,

"Praise God!

Blessings on the one who comes in the name of the Lord!

Hail to the King of Israel!"

14 Jesus found a young donkey and rode on it, fulfilling the prophecy that said:

15 "Don't be afraid, people of Jerusalem.

Look, your King is coming,

riding on a donkey's colt."

16 His disciples didn't understand at the time that this was a fulfillment of prophecy. But after Jesus entered into his glory, they remembered what had happened and realized that these things had been written about him.

17 Many in the crowd had seen Jesus call Lazarus from the tomb, raising him from the dead, and they were telling others about it. 18 That was the reason so many went out to meet him—because they had heard about this miraculous sign. 19 Then the Pharisees said to each other, "There's nothing we can do. Look, everyone has gone after him!"

FYI

Nard was a perfume often used to anoint people for burial. (See the FYI on page 67.)

In verse 13, the crowd was quoting from Psalm 118:26 — "Bless the one who comes in the name of the Lord. We bless you from the house of the Lord."

In verse 15, the author was quoting from Zechariah 9:9 — "Rejoice, O people of Zion! Shout in triumph, O people of Jerusalem! Look, your king is coming to you. He is righteous and victorious, yet he is humble, riding on a donkey — riding on a donkey's colt."

 What do you think of Mary's sacrifice? Why?

What do you think of Judas Iscariot's response? Why?

 Imagine the experience of Lazarus during this time — his death, his resurrection, the visit from Jesus, the curious crowds, and then the plot to kill him (12:10).

Mary believed Jesus when he said he was going to die and rise again, so she willingly prepared him for what was to come. She took this opportunity to minister to Jesus in his time of need, as he had done for her. Perhaps the fragrance of this perfume could be smelled as Jesus was on the cross, a gentle reminder of how at least one person had honored and worshipped Jesus in his final days.

Dear God — May I be someone who always welcomes and worships King Jesus into my life, my thoughts, my attitudes, and my actions.

71

Jesus Predicts
His Death

20 Some Greeks who had come to Jerusalem for the Passover celebration 21 paid a visit to Philip, who was from Bethsaida in Galilee. They said, "Sir, we want to meet Jesus." 22 Philip told Andrew about it, and they went together to ask Jesus.

23 Jesus replied, *"Now the time has come for the Son of Man to enter into his glory. 24 I tell you the truth, unless a kernel of wheat is planted in the soil and dies, it remains alone. But its death will produce many new kernels–a plentiful harvest of new lives. 25 Those who love their life in this world will lose it. Those who care nothing for their life in this world will keep it for eternity. 26 Anyone who wants to serve me must follow me, because my servants must be where I am. And the Father will honor anyone who serves me.*

27 *"Now my soul is deeply troubled. Should I pray, 'Father, save me from this hour'? But this is the very reason I came! 28 Father, bring glory to your name."*

Then a voice spoke from heaven, saying, "I have already brought glory to my name, and I will do so again." 29 When the crowd heard the voice, some thought it was thunder, while others declared an angel had spoken to him.

30 Then Jesus told them, *"The voice was for your benefit, not mine. 31 The time for judging this world has come, when Satan, the ruler of this world, will be cast out. 32 And when I am lifted up from the earth, I will draw everyone to myself."* 33 He said this to indicate how he was going to die.

34 The crowd responded, "We understood from Scripture that the Messiah would live forever. How can you say the Son of Man will die? Just who is this Son of Man, anyway?"

35 Jesus replied, *"My light will shine for you just a little longer. Walk in the light while you can, so the darkness will not overtake you. Those who walk in the darkness cannot see where they are going. 36 Put your trust in the light while there is still time; then you will become children of the light."*

After saying these things, Jesus went away and was hidden from them.

The Unbelief
of the People

37 But despite all the miraculous signs Jesus had done, most of the people still did not believe in him. 38 This is exactly what Isaiah the prophet had predicted:

"Lord, who has believed our message?
To whom has the Lord revealed his powerful arm?"

FYI

The Greek word for **satan** means "the adversary." It doesn't appear in this verse in the original Greek manuscripts, which says "... the prince/ruler of this world will be cast out."

Son of Man was a name Jesus used for himself, and a name that Old Testament prophets used for a future savior and ruler. You can read more about this in earlier FYIs.

Isaiah 53:1 says, "Who has believed our message? To whom has the Lord revealed his powerful arm?"

What do you think Jesus meant when he said these things:

Those who love their life in the world will lose it.

Those who care nothing for their life in this world will keep it for eternity.

Anyone who wants to serve me must follow me, because my servants must be where I am.

Copy verse 36 here. Spend some time thinking about what it means to become "children of the light."

Were you ever afraid of the dark? How refreshing light is in the moments when we cannot see. Jesus came to shine as Light in the Darkness. He illuminates love, peace, and comfort in the darkness of our lives. He wants to heal the broken, dislocated parts of our world that need to be put back together. Jesus wants us to see clearly — not only the world, but also ourselves — through his miraculous, refreshing, never-ending light! Where do you need to see clearly today?

Dear God — Thank you that when Jesus' soul was troubled about his coming death, he willingly went forward with his mission to die for all of humanity. Thank you for his priceless sacrifice.

₃₉ But the people couldn't believe, for as Isaiah also said,

₄₀ "The Lord has blinded their eyes

and hardened their hearts—

so that their eyes cannot see,

and their hearts cannot understand,

and they cannot turn to me

and have me heal them."

₄₁ Isaiah was referring to Jesus when he said this, because he saw the future and spoke of the Messiah's glory. ₄₂ Many people did believe in him, however, including some of the Jewish leaders. But they wouldn't admit it for fear that the Pharisees would expel them from the synagogue. ₄₃ For they loved human praise more than the praise of God.

₄₄ Jesus shouted to the crowds, *"If you trust me, you are trusting not only me, but also God who sent me. ₄₅ For when you see me, you are seeing the one who sent me. ₄₆ I have come as a light to shine in this dark world, so that all who put their trust in me will no longer remain in the dark. ₄₇ I will not judge those who hear me but don't obey me, for I have come to save the world and not to judge it. ₄₈ But all who reject me and my message will be judged on the day of judgment by the truth I have spoken. ₄₉ I don't speak on my own authority. The Father who sent me has commanded me what to say and how to say it. ₅₀ And I know his commands lead to eternal life; so I say whatever the Father tells me to say."*

Jesus Washes His Disciples' Feet

CHAPTER 13　Before the Passover celebration, Jesus knew that his hour had come to leave this world and return to his Father. He had loved his disciples during his ministry on earth, and now he loved them to the very end. ₂ It was time for supper, and the devil had already prompted Judas, son of Simon Iscariot, to betray Jesus. ₃ Jesus knew that the Father had given him authority over everything and that he had come from God and would return to God. ₄ So he got up from the table, took off his robe, wrapped a towel around his waist, ₅ and poured water into a basin. Then he began to wash the disciples' feet, drying them with the towel he had around him.

₆ When Jesus came to Simon Peter, Peter said to him, "Lord, are you going to wash my feet?"

₇ Jesus replied, *"You don't understand now what I am doing, but someday you will."*

Foot washing was common in the ancient world where people wore sandals on dusty roads. Hosts sometimes washed the feet of guests as a sign of hospitality. Foot washing was also an expression of honor and servitude (for example, servants to masters or parents to children).

The Greek word for **devil** is "diabolos." It refers to someone who slanders, accuses falsely, or opposes the plans and purposes of God. Jesus was tempted in the wilderness by diabolos (Matthew 4, Luke 4).

Do you think some people today believe in Jesus but are afraid to admit it? Why?

Why do you think Jesus washed his disciples' feet?

Jesus was confident about his purpose (13:1) and his identity (13:3). Think about your life as a follower of Jesus and write these things here:

My Identity

My Purpose

Jesus knew his true identity: he knew who his Father was, he knew the Father had given him authority, he knew that he had been sent by God, and he knew that he would return to God. Jesus was absolutely confident about who he was and what his purpose was. Because of that, he could act with confidence and hope. Followers of Jesus can know their identity (they are in Christ, adopted as God's beloved children) and their purpose (to faithfully follow Jesus in every way, every day).

Dear God — Thank you for the example of Jesus' humility. Please help me be someone who does not love human praise more than the praise of God, and who willingly serves others.

8 "No," Peter protested, "you will never ever wash my feet!"

Jesus replied, *"Unless I wash you, you won't belong to me."*

9 Simon Peter exclaimed, "Then wash my hands and head as well, Lord, not just my feet!"

10 Jesus replied, *"A person who has bathed all over does not need to wash, except for the feet, to be entirely clean. And you disciples are clean, but not all of you."* 11 For Jesus knew who would betray him. That is what he meant when he said, *"Not all of you are clean."*

12 After washing their feet, he put on his robe again and sat down and asked, *"Do you understand what I was doing? 13 You call me 'Teacher' and 'Lord,' and you are right, because that's what I am. 14 And since I, your Lord and Teacher, have washed your feet, you ought to wash each other's feet. 15 I have given you an example to follow. Do as I have done to you. 16 I tell you the truth, slaves are not greater than their master. Nor is the messenger more important than the one who sends the message. 17 Now that you know these things, God will bless you for doing them.*

Jesus Predicts His Betrayal

18 *"I am not saying these things to all of you; I know the ones I have chosen. But this fulfills the Scripture that says, 'The one who eats my food has turned against me.' 19 I tell you this beforehand, so that when it happens you will believe that I am the Messiah. 20 I tell you the truth, anyone who welcomes my messenger is welcoming me, and anyone who welcomes me is welcoming the Father who sent me."*

21 Now Jesus was deeply troubled, and he exclaimed, *"I tell you the truth, one of you will betray me!"*

22 The disciples looked at each other, wondering whom he could mean. 23 The disciple Jesus loved was sitting next to Jesus at the table. 24 Simon Peter motioned to him to ask, "Who's he talking about?" 25 So that disciple leaned over to Jesus and asked, "Lord, who is it?"

26 Jesus responded, *"It is the one to whom I give the bread I dip in the bowl."* And when he had dipped it, he gave it to Judas, son of Simon Iscariot. 27 When Judas had eaten the bread, Satan entered into him. Then Jesus told him, *"Hurry and do what you're going to do."* 28 None of the others at the table knew what Jesus meant. 29 Since Judas was their treasurer, some thought Jesus was telling him to go and pay for the food or to give some money to the poor. 30 So Judas left at once, going out into the night.

FYI

The disciple Jesus loved (verse 23) was probably John, whose experiences and memories are the basis for the gospel named after him.

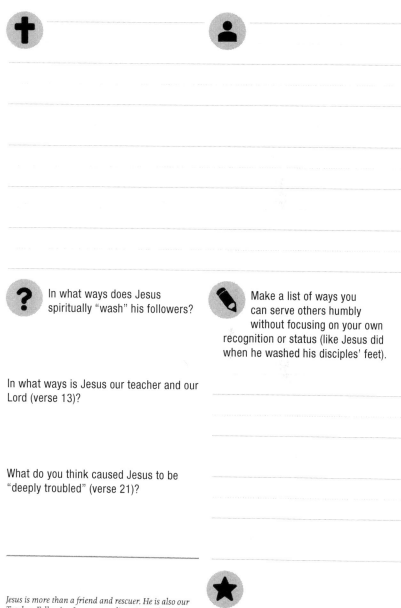

In what ways does Jesus spiritually "wash" his followers?

In what ways is Jesus our teacher and our Lord (verse 13)?

What do you think caused Jesus to be "deeply troubled" (verse 21)?

Make a list of ways you can serve others humbly without focusing on your own recognition or status (like Jesus did when he washed his disciples' feet).

Jesus is more than a friend and rescuer. He is also our Teacher. Following Jesus means listening to, learning from, and living out his teaching every day. And he is our Lord and King. Following Jesus means trusting, worshipping, obeying, and surrendering to our King every day.

Dear God — Help me be a loyal and faithful follower of you. Protect me against any temptation to forget you, ignore you, or betray you.

31 As soon as Judas left the room, Jesus said, *"The time has come for the Son of Man to enter into his glory, and God will be glorified because of him. 32 And since God receives glory because of the Son, he will give his own glory to the Son, and he will do so at once. 33 Dear children, I will be with you only a little longer. And as I told the Jewish leaders, you will search for me, but you can't come where I am going. 34 So now I am giving you a new commandment: Love each other. Just as I have loved you, you should love each other. 35 Your love for one another will prove to the world that you are my disciples."*

36 Simon Peter asked, "Lord, where are you going?"

And Jesus replied, *"You can't go with me now, but you will follow me later."*

37 "But why can't I come now, Lord?" he asked. "I'm ready to die for you."

38 Jesus answered, *"Die for me? I tell you the truth, Peter—before the rooster crows tomorrow morning, you will deny three times that you even know me.*

CHAPTER 14 *"Don't let your hearts be troubled. Trust in God, and trust also in me. 2 There is more than enough room in my Father's home. If this were not so, would I have told you that I am going to prepare a place for you? 3 When everything is ready, I will come and get you, so that you will always be with me where I am. 4 And you know the way to where I am going."*

5 "No, we don't know, Lord," Thomas said. "We have no idea where you are going, so how can we know the way?"

6 Jesus told him, *"I am the way, the truth, and the life. No one can come to the Father except through me. 7 If you had really known me, you would know who my Father is. From now on, you do know him and have seen him!"*

8 Philip said, "Lord, show us the Father, and we will be satisfied."

9 Jesus replied, *"Have I been with you all this time, Philip, and yet you still don't know who I am? Anyone who has seen me has seen the Father! So why are you asking me to show him to you? 10 Don't you believe that I am in the Father and the Father is in me? The words I speak are not my own, but my Father who lives in me does his work through me.*

11 *"Just believe that I am in the Father and the Father is in me. Or at least believe because of the work you have seen me do. 12 I tell you the truth, anyone who believes*

FYI

*John 14-17 is sometimes called the **Farewell Discourse** (because these are Jesus' last words to his disciples before his arrest) or the **Upper Room Discourse** (because that is where Jesus spoke these words).*

***Glory** has several meanings in Scripture. Sometimes it refers to a visible blaze of light and splendor (for example, when angels appear to humans, or when Jesus was transformed on the mountaintop). Sometimes it refers to praise and worship of God. Sometimes it refers to the honor and respect that God deserves. Romans 8 says that because followers of Jesus are adopted as God's children, we will inherit God's glory just as Jesus did (see Romans 8:15-30).*

In what ways have you been faithful and loyal to Jesus? In what ways have you denied or been unfaithful to Jesus? How can you grow to be a more faithful and loyal follower of Christ?

What things "trouble your heart" (14:1)? How will you trust Jesus more and more with those things?

What do you think Jesus meant when he said "no one can come to the Father except through me"?

Copy verses 34-35 here. Think about ways that you will love all other followers of Jesus.

*Even if you believe, love, and follow God, there may be days when he feels distant. When that happens, some people simply walk away. They think how they feel about God is more important than what is true about God. Other people go into overdrive, trying to reconnect with God by being more "spiritual" or "good." There is only one way to God: JESUS. He **reconciles** us to God, **reveals** God to us, and makes it possible for us to **remain** in and with God. Jesus is the way, truth, and life. Look for God by looking at Jesus. (John 14:6)*

★

Dear God — Thank you for providing a way to God, your Father. Help me to stay focused on you as the only source of truth and life.

in me will do the same works I have done, and even greater works, because I am going to be with the Father. 13 You can ask for anything in my name, and I will do it, so that the Son can bring glory to the Father. 14 Yes, ask me for anything in my name, and I will do it!

Jesus Promises the Holy Spirit

15 "If you love me, obey my commandments. 16 And I will ask the Father, and he will give you another Advocate, who will never leave you. 17 He is the Holy Spirit, who leads into all truth. The world cannot receive him, because it isn't looking for him and doesn't recognize him. But you know him, because he lives with you now and later will be in you.

18 "No, I will not abandon you as orphans–I will come to you. 19 Soon the world will no longer see me, but you will see me. Since I live, you also will live. 20 When I am raised to life again, you will know that I am in my Father, and you are in me, and I am in you. 21 Those who accept my commandments and obey them are the ones who love me. And because they love me, my Father will love them. And I will love them and reveal myself to each of them."

22 Judas (not Judas Iscariot, but the other disciple with that name) said to him, "Lord, why are you going to reveal yourself only to us and not to the world at large?"

23 Jesus replied, "All who love me will do what I say. My Father will love them, and we will come and make our home with each of them. 24 Anyone who doesn't love me will not obey me.

"And remember, my words are not my own. What I am telling you is from the Father who sent me. 25 I am telling you these things now while I am still with you. 26 But when the Father sends the Advocate as my representative–that is, the Holy Spirit–he will teach you everything and will remind you of everything I have told you.

27 "I am leaving you with a gift–peace of mind and heart. And the peace I give is a gift the world cannot give. So don't be troubled or afraid. 28 Remember what I told you: I am going away, but I will come back to you again. If you really loved me, you would be happy that I am going to the Father, who is greater than I am. 29 I have told you these things before they happen so that when they do happen, you will believe.

30 "I don't have much more time to talk to you, because the ruler of this world approaches. He has no power over me, 31 but I will do what the Father requires of me, so that the world will know that I love the Father. Come, let's be going."

FYI

What have you heard or been taught about the Holy Spirit? What things do you want to learn and understand about the Holy Spirit?

Why do you think Jesus so often connects love and obedience (as in verses 21, 23-24)?

Create a symbol or image that "shows" how Jesus is in the Father, how we are in Jesus, and how Jesus is in us (verse 20; also in John 15:1-11).

Jesus is always with his followers. He gives his Spirit to fill our hearts and be with us every moment of every day. He doesn't leave us, abandon us, forget us, get tired of us, or give up on us. Even when we are by ourselves, we are never really alone. God is there. Jesus is with us. The Spirit is in us.

Dear God — I want to love you more and more each day. Help me to be your obedient and loving child in all my thoughts, words, and actions.

CHAPTER 15   *"I am the true grapevine, and my Father is the gardener. 2 He cuts off every branch of mine that doesn't produce fruit, and he prunes the branches that do bear fruit so they will produce even more. 3 You have already been pruned and purified by the message I have given you. 4 Remain in me, and I will remain in you. For a branch cannot produce fruit if it is severed from the vine, and you cannot be fruitful unless you remain in me.*

5 "Yes, I am the vine; you are the branches. Those who remain in me, and I in them, will produce much fruit. For apart from me you can do nothing. 6 Anyone who does not remain in me is thrown away like a useless branch and withers. Such branches are gathered into a pile to be burned. 7 But if you remain in me and my words remain in you, you may ask for anything you want, and it will be granted! 8 When you produce much fruit, you are my true disciples. This brings great glory to my Father.

9 "I have loved you even as the Father has loved me. Remain in my love. 10 When you obey my commandments, you remain in my love, just as I obey my Father's commandments and remain in his love. 11 I have told you these things so that you will be filled with my joy. Yes, your joy will overflow! 12 This is my commandment: Love each other in the same way I have loved you. 13 There is no greater love than to lay down one's life for one's friends. 14 You are my friends if you do what I command. 15 I no longer call you slaves, because a master doesn't confide in his slaves. Now you are my friends, since I have told you everything the Father told me. 16 You didn't choose me. I chose you. I appointed you to go and produce lasting fruit, so that the Father will give you whatever you ask for, using my name. 17 This is my command: Love each other.

18 "If the world hates you, remember that it hated me first. 19 The world would love you as one of its own if you belonged to it, but you are no longer part of the world. I chose you to come out of the world, so it hates you. 20 Do you remember what I told you? 'A slave is not greater than the master.' Since they persecuted me, naturally they will persecute you. And if they had listened to me, they would listen to you. 21 They will do all this to you because of me, for they have rejected the one who sent me. 22 They would not be guilty if I had not come and spoken to them. But now they have no excuse for their sin. 23 Anyone who hates me also hates my Father. 24 If I hadn't done such miraculous signs among them that no one else could do, they would not be guilty. But as it is, they have seen everything I did, yet they still hate me and my Father.

FYI

Many people consider John 15 to be one of the most beautiful passages in the Bible.

*In the Old Testament, the people of God (Israel) are often described as a **vine**. When the people were obedient and faithful, they were pictured as a healthy and fruitful vine. When they worshipped idols and turned their back on God, they were pictured as a withered, wild, or dying vine.*

*The word **remain** is also translated as **abide**.*

 List all the things Jesus says about the vine.

List all the things Jesus says about the branches.

What do those things teach us about Jesus and his followers?

Jesus is the true vine. Think about the untrue/false things that you go to for life, identity, meaning, and happiness. Write down one way that you will stay connected to Jesus every day.

What is your favorite fruit? In a recent year, the top selling fruit was bananas. Jesus compares Christians to trees designed to produce fruit. The best fruit emerging from Christians is love. The best way to water the tree is to know and follow God's Word. Do you want to know God's love and give it to others? If so, keep learning Jesus' teachings — just like you are doing now — and then put them into action.

Dear God — Help me to remain and abide in Jesus more and more each day. Help me to live in a way that brings you glory.

25 *"This fulfills what is written in their Scriptures: 'They hated me without cause.'*

26 *"But I will send you the Advocate–the Spirit of truth. He will come to you from the Father and will testify all about me. 27 And you must also testify about me because you have been with me from the beginning of my ministry.*

CHAPTER 16 *"I have told you these things so that you won't abandon your faith. 2 For you will be expelled from the synagogues, and the time is coming when those who kill you will think they are doing a holy service for God. 3 This is because they have never known the Father or me. 4 Yes, I'm telling you these things now, so that when they happen, you will remember my warning. I didn't tell you earlier because I was going to be with you for a while longer.*

The Work of the Holy Spirit

5 *"But now I am going away to the one who sent me, and not one of you is asking where I am going. 6 Instead, you grieve because of what I've told you. 7 But in fact, it is best for you that I go away, because if I don't, the Advocate won't come. If I do go away, then I will send him to you. 8 And when he comes, he will convict the world of its sin, and of God's righteousness, and of the coming judgment. 9 The world's sin is that it refuses to believe in me. 10 Righteousness is available because I go to the Father, and you will see me no more. 11 Judgment will come because the ruler of this world has already been judged.*

12 *"There is so much more I want to tell you, but you can't bear it now. 13 When the Spirit of truth comes, he will guide you into all truth. He will not speak on his own but will tell you what he has heard. He will tell you about the future. 14 He will bring me glory by telling you whatever he receives from me. 15 All that belongs to the Father is mine; this is why I said, 'The Spirit will tell you whatever he receives from me.' "In a little while you won't see me anymore. But a little while after that, you will see me again."*

17 Some of the disciples asked each other, "What does he mean when he says, 'In a little while you won't see me, but then you will see me,' and 'I am going to the Father'? 18 And what does he mean by 'a little while'? We don't understand."

19 Jesus realized they wanted to ask him about it, so he said, *"Are you asking yourselves what I meant? I said in a little while you won't see me, but a little while after that you will see me again. 20 I tell you the truth, you will weep and mourn over what is going to happen to me, but the world will rejoice. You will grieve, but your grief will*

FYI

Righteousness means being as we ought to be, being acceptable to God, living rightly. Jesus' death and resurrection makes it possible for people to be made right with God. He forgives. He washes away the stain of sin. He gives us a new heart and his Holy Spirit that helps us to love, follow, and obey him.

Here are some verses about righteousness (both being made right with God and living rightly):

Romans 3:22

Romans 6:13-18

Romans 8:10

1 Corinthians 1:30

2 Corinthians 5:21

Ephesians 4:24

Philippians 1:11

2 Timothy 3:16

1 Peter 3:14

2 Peter 3:13

1 John 3:7-10

? What do you think it means to abandon your faith (16:1)? Why do you think some people do this?

Why did Jesus say it was good for him to go away (verse 7)? What do you think he meant?

What do you notice about Jesus (God the Son), the Father, and the Spirit in verses 12-16?

Write down one way you have experienced, sensed, or heard the Holy Spirit (Christ's Spirit in you).

What a gift the Holy Spirit is! He always speaks the truth. He speaks words from God the Father. He points to Jesus the Son and honors him. The Spirit is the great connector, connecting followers of Jesus to God. Let us all pay more attention to what the Spirit is showing and teaching us about God.

Dear God — Help me to experience and listen to your Spirit living in me. Help me learn from him, be comforted by him, and be guided by him.

85

suddenly turn to wonderful joy. 21 It will be like a woman suffering the pains of labor. When her child is born, her anguish gives way to joy because she has brought a new baby into the world. 22 So you have sorrow now, but I will see you again; then you will rejoice, and no one can rob you of that joy. 23 At that time you won't need to ask me for anything. I tell you the truth, you will ask the Father directly, and he will grant your request because you use my name. 24 You haven't done this before. Ask, using my name, and you will receive, and you will have abundant joy.

25 "I have spoken of these matters in figures of speech, but soon I will stop speaking figuratively and will tell you plainly all about the Father. 26 Then you will ask in my name. I'm not saying I will ask the Father on your behalf, 27 for the Father himself loves you dearly because you love me and believe that I came from God. 28 Yes, I came from the Father into the world, and now I will leave the world and return to the Father."

29 Then his disciples said, "At last you are speaking plainly and not figuratively. 30 Now we understand that you know everything, and there's no need to question you. From this we believe that you came from God."

31 Jesus asked, "Do you finally believe? 32 But the time is coming–indeed it's here now–when you will be scattered, each one going his own way, leaving me alone. Yet I am not alone because the Father is with me. 33 I have told you all this so that you may have peace in me. Here on earth you will have many trials and sorrows. But take heart, because I have overcome the world."

The Prayer of Jesus **CHAPTER 17** After saying all these things, Jesus looked up to heaven and said, "Father, the hour has come. Glorify your Son so he can give glory back to you. 2 For you have given him authority over everyone. He gives eternal life to each one you have given him. 3 And this is the way to have eternal life–to know you, the only true God, and Jesus Christ, the one you sent to earth. 4 I brought glory to you here on earth by completing the work you gave me to do. 5 Now, Father, bring me into the glory we shared before the world began.

6 "I have revealed you to the ones you gave me from this world. They were always yours. You gave them to me, and they have kept your word. 7 Now they know that everything I have is a gift from you, 8 for I have passed on to them the message you gave me. They accepted it and know that I came from you, and they believe you sent me.

The Bible uses birth descriptions and imagery in many different places. One of the results of sin was that childbirth became difficult (so did farming, or working the land — see Genesis 3 for more about this). The book of Job (chapter 38) says that at creation the sea burst from the womb; that God gives birth to the morning dew, ice, and frost. In chapter 39, the book of Job says that God knows when wild animals give birth. In John 3, Jesus described following him as being born again. Romans 8 says that all creation was affected by sin so it groans with the pains of childbirth (but someday will be created anew, just like God's people).

At first glance, it might seem like Jesus said that people will get whatever they ask for in prayer (go back and look at 15:7 and see 17:24). But it's important to know all that the Bible says about prayer. Many obedient people in the Bible did not receive what they asked for. Read Luke 22:39-44 to learn about Jesus' own experience with this. What do you think Jesus was teaching about prayer in these verses of John? (Also check out Romans 8:26-27.)

What is one thing you are faithfully praying for, in the name of Jesus, in agreement with God's will?

Jesus told his disciples that they would face many trials and sorrows. The same is true for his followers today. The world is not especially welcoming to God, Jesus, the cross, or the invitation to surrender ourselves and receive new life. But: take heart because Jesus has overcome the world! Because of his death and resurrection, and the gift of the Holy Spirit, we can face trials and sorrows with his supernatural peace. Trials and sorrows don't disappear for followers of Jesus — but we never face them alone because of Jesus.

Dear God — Teach me to pray as Jesus prayed. Help me to pray honestly, from my heart, and also humbly, believing that your will and your plans are the best for me.

9 *"My prayer is not for the world, but for those you have given me, because they belong to you. 10 All who are mine belong to you, and you have given them to me, so they bring me glory. 11 Now I am departing from the world; they are staying in this world, but I am coming to you. Holy Father, you have given me your name; now protect them by the power of your name so that they will be united just as we are. 12 During my time here, I protected them by the power of the name you gave me. I guarded them so that not one was lost, except the one headed for destruction, as the Scriptures foretold.*

13 *"Now I am coming to you. I told them many things while I was with them in this world so they would be filled with my joy. 14 I have given them your word. And the world hates them because they do not belong to the world, just as I do not belong to the world. 15 I'm not asking you to take them out of the world, but to keep them safe from the evil one. 16 They do not belong to this world any more than I do. 17 Make them holy by your truth; teach them your word, which is truth. 18 Just as you sent me into the world, I am sending them into the world. 19 And I give myself as a holy sacrifice for them so they can be made holy by your truth.*

20 *"I am praying not only for these disciples but also for all who will ever believe in me through their message. 21 I pray that they will all be one, just as you and I are one—as you are in me, Father, and I am in you. And may they be in us so that the world will believe you sent me.*

22 *"I have given them the glory you gave me, so they may be one as we are one. 23 I am in them and you are in me. May they experience such perfect unity that the world will know that you sent me and that you love them as much as you love me. 24 Father, I want these whom you have given me to be with me where I am. Then they can see all the glory you gave me because you loved me even before the world began!*

25 *"O righteous Father, the world doesn't know you, but I do; and these disciples know you sent me. 26 I have revealed you to them, and I will continue to do so. Then your love for me will be in them, and I will be in them."*

Jesus is Betrayed and Arrested

CHAPTER 18   After saying these things, Jesus crossed the Kidron Valley with his disciples and entered a grove of olive trees. 2 Judas, the betrayer, knew this place, because Jesus had often gone there with his disciples. 3 The leading priests and Pharisees had given Judas a contingent of Roman soldiers and Temple guards to accompany him.

FYI

What are your thoughts about the things Jesus prayed for?

In verse 20, Jesus prayed for you. Respond to that here in words or images.

What things seem especially important to Jesus in his prayer?

Jesus was facing betrayal and death. At that moment he was thinking about his current friends and praying for us, his future friends and disciples! Knowing and believing that Jesus prays for, protects, and loves us increases our ability to do hard things. Knowing and believing we are completely loved by Jesus makes it possible to do what feels impossible. When people see us truly living as the beloved of God, we reflect his glory.

Dear God — Thank you that even before I was born, Jesus prayed for me. Help me to be one with other Christ followers, as Jesus prayed. Help me to remain in you so that others will believe in Jesus, just as he prayed.

89

Now with blazing torches, lanterns, and weapons, they arrived at the olive grove.

4 Jesus fully realized all that was going to happen to him, so he stepped forward to meet them. *"Who are you looking for?"* he asked.

5 "Jesus the Nazarene," they replied.

"I am he," Jesus said. (Judas, who betrayed him, was standing with them.) 6 As Jesus said *"I AM he,"* they all drew back and fell to the ground! 7 Once more he asked them, *"Who are you looking for?"*

And again they replied, "Jesus the Nazarene."

8 *"I told you that I am he,"* Jesus said. *"And since I am the one you want, let these others go."* 9 He did this to fulfill his own statement: *"I did not lose a single one of those you have given me."*

10 Then Simon Peter drew a sword and slashed off the right ear of Malchus, the high priest's slave. 11 But Jesus said to Peter, *"Put your sword back into its sheath. Shall I not drink from the cup of suffering the Father has given me?"*

Jesus at the High Priest's House

12 So the soldiers, their commanding officer, and the Temple guards arrested Jesus and tied him up. 13 First they took him to Annas, since he was the father-in-law of Caiaphas, the high priest at that time. 14 Caiaphas was the one who had told the other Jewish leaders, "It's better that one man should die for the people."

Peter's First Denial

15 Simon Peter followed Jesus, as did another of the disciples. That other disciple was acquainted with the high priest, so he was allowed to enter the high priest's courtyard with Jesus. 16 Peter had to stay outside the gate. Then the disciple who knew the high priest spoke to the woman watching at the gate, and she let Peter in. 17 The woman asked Peter, "You're not one of that man's disciples, are you?"

"No," he said, "I am not."

18 Because it was cold, the household servants and the guards had made a charcoal fire. They stood around it, warming themselves, and Peter stood with them, warming himself.

The High Priest Questions Jesus

19 Inside, the high priest began asking Jesus about his followers and what he had been teaching them. 20 Jesus replied, *"Everyone knows what I teach. I have preached regularly in the synagogues and the Temple, where the people gather. I have not spoken in secret. 21 Why are you asking me this question? Ask those who heard me. They know what I said."*

FYI

All the accounts of Jesus' life tell the story of **Malchus's** ear being cut off. But only John names him. Only Luke (who was a physician) tells us that Jesus healed the man's ear (Luke 22:51).

Some people believe the **unnamed disciple** in verses 15-16 might have been Nicodemus. Many other people believe it was John himself.

Historians tell us that **Annas** had been the Jewish high priest from A.D. 6-15. According to Bible scholars, the place where Jesus cleared the Temple was known as the "Bazaar (marketplace) of Annas" because he profited from the overpriced sales of sacrificial animals.

Jesus wasn't being rude or disrespectful when responding to the high priest starting in verse 20. Jewish custom was that prisoners couldn't be charged or convicted based on their answers to incriminating questions. That's why Jesus said, "Ask those who saw me and heard me."

? Why do you think Jesus so quickly and willingly identified himself to the soldiers and guards?

Imagine being present at the events of this night. How do you think you might have felt and responded?

Make a list of ways you understand and relate to Peter.

Peter was one of Jesus' closest and dearest friends — and also one of the most impulsive. What exactly did he think he would accomplish with one sword against a whole contingency of soldiers? He wasn't even very good with that sword — an EAR?! Peter didn't like what was happening. So he stepped in. Jesus stopped Peter and pointed him back to the truth, reminding him that we must not interfere with the Father's plans.

Dear God — I do not understand your willingness to face death on behalf of all humanity. Help me to understand the depth of your humble sacrifice.

22 Then one of the Temple guards standing nearby slapped Jesus across the face. "Is that the way to answer the high priest?" he demanded.

23 Jesus replied, *"If I said anything wrong, you must prove it. But if I'm speaking the truth, why are you beating me?"*

24 Then Annas bound Jesus and sent him to Caiaphas, the high priest.

Peter's Second and Third Denial

25 Meanwhile, as Simon Peter was standing by the fire warming himself, they asked him again, "You're not one of his disciples, are you?"

He denied it, saying, "No, I am not."

26 But one of the household slaves of the high priest, a relative of the man whose ear Peter had cut off, asked, "Didn't I see you out there in the olive grove with Jesus?"

27 Again Peter denied it. And immediately a rooster crowed.

Jesus' Trial

28 Jesus' trial before Caiaphas ended in the early hours of the morning. Then he was taken to the headquarters of the Roman governor. His accusers didn't go inside because it would defile them, and they wouldn't be allowed to celebrate the Passover.

29 So Pilate, the governor, went out to them and asked, "What is your charge against this man?"

30 "We wouldn't have handed him over to you if he weren't a criminal!" they retorted.

31 "Then take him away and judge him by your own law," Pilate told them.

"Only the Romans are permitted to execute someone," the Jewish leaders replied 32 (This fulfilled Jesus' prediction about the way he would die.)

33 Then Pilate went back into his headquarters and called for Jesus to be brought to him. "Are you the king of the Jews?" he asked him.

34 Jesus replied, *"Is this your own question, or did others tell you about me?"*

35 "Am I a Jew?" Pilate retorted. "Your own people and their leading priests brought you to me for trial. Why? What have you done?"

36 Jesus answered, *"My Kingdom is not an earthly kingdom. If it were, my followers would fight to keep me from being handed over to the Jewish leaders. But my Kingdom is not of this world."*

37 Pilate said, "So you are a king?"

FYI

Pilate was the Roman governor of Judea. He was part of the foreign occupying power. The Jewish leaders retained some control, but they were not allowed to issue a death penalty. Only Pilate could do that.

Pilate was a Gentile (non-Jew). According to Jewish law, entering a Gentile home would **defile** a person, making them ceremonially unclean.

Jesus often spoke about the **Kingdom** of God, which he initiated through his life, death, and resurrection, and over which he rules forever. Colossians 1:13 says that God has rescued followers of Jesus from the kingdom of darkness and transferred them into the Kingdom of his dear Son.

 What things are true about earthly kingdoms? How is that like God's Kingdom?

How is Jesus like and unlike an earthly king?

What are your impressions of Peter? of Jesus' accusers? of Pilate? of Jesus?

 Describe a perfect Kingdom and a perfect King.

Sometimes it might seem easier to deny Jesus than to follow him. Being a follower of Jesus can be challenging, uncomfortable, and costly. But the challenge, discomfort, and cost are always worth it because he is the loving Messiah, the good King, and the powerful Savior. If you are tempted to deny Jesus, cling tightly to him, and set your eyes on him, remembering how faithful he is to his undeserving followers. He never denies knowing us or loving us.

Dear God — Thank you for establishing your Kingdom and for allowing followers of Jesus to be part of it. Help me to honor, follow, trust, and serve Jesus as my King.

Jesus responded, *"You say I am a king. Actually, I was born and came into the world to testify to the truth. All who love the truth recognize that what I say is true."*

38 "What is truth?" Pilate asked. Then he went out again to the people and told them, "He is not guilty of any crime. 39 But you have a custom of asking me to release one prisoner each year at Passover. Would you like me to release this 'King of the Jews'?"

40 But they shouted back, "No! Not this man. We want Barabbas!" (Barabbas was a revolutionary.)

Jesus Sentenced to Death

CHAPTER 19   Then Pilate had Jesus flogged with a lead-tipped whip. 2 The soldiers wove a crown of thorns and put it on his head, and they put a purple robe on him. 3 "Hail! King of the Jews!" they mocked, as they slapped him across the face.

4 Pilate went outside again and said to the people, "I am going to bring him out to you now, but understand clearly that I find him not guilty." 5 Then Jesus came out wearing the crown of thorns and the purple robe. And Pilate said, "Look, here is the man!"

6 When they saw him, the leading priests and Temple guards began shouting, "Crucify him! Crucify him!"

"Take him yourselves and crucify him," Pilate said. "I find him not guilty."

7 The Jewish leaders replied, "By our law he ought to die because he called himself the Son of God."

8 When Pilate heard this, he was more frightened than ever. 9 He took Jesus back into the headquarters again and asked him, "Where are you from?" But Jesus gave no answer. 10 "Why don't you talk to me?" Pilate demanded. "Don't you realize that I have the power to release you or crucify you?"

11 Then Jesus said, *"You would have no power over me at all unless it were given to you from above. So the one who handed me over to you has the greater sin."*

12 Then Pilate tried to release him, but the Jewish leaders shouted, "If you release this man, you are no 'friend of Caesar.' Anyone who declares himself a king is a rebel against Caesar."

13 When they said this, Pilate brought Jesus out to them again. Then Pilate sat down on the judgment seat on the platform that is called the Stone Pavement (in

FYI

Barabbas was most likely a revolutionary — someone who fought against the Roman occupying forces with zealous Jewish loyalty. Ironically, many Jewish people had hoped for a Messiah who would serve as a political and military revolutionary.

Caesar ruled the Roman empire. At the time of Jesus, this included the northern border of Africa (the edge of what's known today as Morocco, Algeria, Tunisia, Libya, and Egypt), the western part of today's Middle East (including Israel, Jordan, Syria, Turkey, parts of Saudi Arabia and Iraq), and the southern portion of today's European countries (including Greece, Bulgaria, Yugoslavia, Croatia, Bosnia, Slovenia, Italy, Switzerland, France, Austria, Belgium, part of Germany, part of Hungary, and part of Romania).

 How do you think Barabbas reacted to what was happening around him?

Why do you think Pilate was so indecisive and conflicted about what to do with Jesus?

Why do you think Jesus responded the way he did to Pilate's questions?

Spend some time thinking about the last hours of Jesus' life. Write your thoughts here.

We are all like Barabbas. We've been unexpectedly and undeservedly released from a death sentence that was totally fair because Jesus willingly paid it on our behalf, which was totally unfair. Jesus is not fair. If he were, we would have all been left trying to find God on our own (impossible), trying to save ourselves on our own (impossible), and trying to figure out life on our own (impossible). Barabbas was set free. So are we. Now live in that freedom.

Dear God — I confess that my sins are connected to Jesus' death. I acknowledge that he suffered ridicule, abuse, beating, and degradation because of me and in defense of me. I owe my life to Jesus, who gave his life for me.

Hebrew, Gabbatha). 14 It was now about noon on the day of preparation for the Passover. And Pilate said to the people, "Look, here is your king!"

15 "Away with him," they yelled. "Away with him! Crucify him!"

"What? Crucify your king?" Pilate asked.

"We have no king but Caesar," the leading priests shouted back.

16 Then Pilate turned Jesus over to them to be crucified.

The Crucifixion

So they took Jesus away. 17 Carrying the cross by himself, he went to the place called Place of the Skull (in Hebrew, Golgotha). 18 There they nailed him to the cross. Two others were crucified with him, one on either side, with Jesus between them. 19 And Pilate posted a sign on the cross that read, "Jesus of Nazareth, the King of the Jews." 20 The place where Jesus was crucified was near the city, and the sign was written in Hebrew, Latin, and Greek, so that many people could read it.

21 Then the leading priests objected and said to Pilate, "Change it from 'The King of the Jews' to 'He said, I am King of the Jews.'"

22 Pilate replied, "No, what I have written, I have written."

23 When the soldiers had crucified Jesus, they divided his clothes among the four of them. They also took his robe, but it was seamless, woven in one piece from top to bottom. 24 So they said, "Rather than tearing it apart, let's throw dice for it." This fulfilled the Scripture that says, "They divided my garments among themselves and threw dice for my clothing." So that is what they did.

Jesus Cares for his Mother

25 Standing near the cross were Jesus' mother, and his mother's sister, Mary (the wife of Clopas), and Mary Magdalene. 26 When Jesus saw his mother standing there beside the disciple he loved, he said to her, *"Dear woman, here is your son."* 27 And he said to this disciple, *"Here is your mother."* And from then on this disciple took her into his home.

The Death of Jesus

28 Jesus knew that his mission was now finished, and to fulfill Scripture he said, *"I am thirsty."* 29 A jar of sour wine was sitting there, so they soaked a sponge in it, put it on a hyssop branch, and held it up to his lips. 30 When Jesus had tasted it, he said, *"It is finished!"* Then he bowed his head and gave up his spirit.

FYI

*We don't know the exact location of the **Place of the Skull**, but it would have been just outside the city walls. It was also called **Golgotha** (the Hebrew form of the word) and **Calvary** (the Latin form of the word).*

__Hebrew, Latin,__ and __Greek__ were the three main languages in Jesus' culture.

Exodus 28 describes all the clothing of a Hebrew priest. Verse 31 dictates that he should wear a __seamless robe, woven in one piece,__ like Jesus' robe.

According to Matthew and Mark, Jesus' __mother's sister__ (the mother of James and John) was named Salome (pronounced: suhLOHmay).

At the first Passover, God's people were protected by marking their homes with the blood of a sacrificed lamb, brushed on the doorframes with a bundle of __hyssop branches__ (Exodus 12:22).

What do you notice most about Jesus in the final hours of his life, as he was on the cross?

The phrase, "It is finished!" is just one word in the original language: tetelestai (pronounced: teh-TEH-less-tie), which is written like this in the original language: τετέλεσται. Write the English phrase or the original word here, thanking God that Jesus' saving work IS FINISHED.

Jesus Christ — God in flesh, perfect in all ways, gentle and kind, wise and loving, strong and good — died for you, died for us, died for the world. Remember Christ's death today. Don't brush it aside. Remember it and be thankful. Remember it and rejoice.

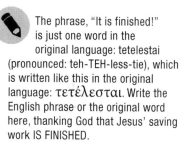

Dear God — Thank you for sending Jesus to rescue humanity. Thank you for sending Jesus to finish the work that was necessary to save us all.

The Burial of Jesus

31 It was the day of preparation, and the Jewish leaders didn't want the bodies hanging there the next day, which was the Sabbath (and a very special Sabbath, because it was Passover week). So they asked Pilate to hasten their deaths by ordering that their legs be broken. Then their bodies could be taken down. 32 So the soldiers came and broke the legs of the two men crucified with Jesus. 33 But when they came to Jesus, they saw that he was already dead, so they didn't break his legs. 34 One of the soldiers, however, pierced his side with a spear, and immediately blood and water flowed out.

35 (This report is from an eyewitness giving an accurate account. He speaks the truth so that you also may continue to believe.) 36 These things happened in fulfillment of the Scriptures that say, "Not one of his bones will be broken," 37 and "They will look on the one they pierced."

38 Afterward Joseph of Arimathea, who had been a secret disciple of Jesus (because he feared the Jewish leaders), asked Pilate for permission to take down Jesus' body. When Pilate gave permission, Joseph came and took the body away. 39 With him came Nicodemus, the man who had come to Jesus at night. He brought about seventy-five pounds of perfumed ointment made from myrrh and aloes. 40 Following Jewish burial custom, they wrapped Jesus' body with the spices in long sheets of linen cloth. 41 The place of crucifixion was near a garden, where there was a new tomb, never used before. 42 And so, because it was the day of preparation for the Jewish Passover and since the tomb was close at hand, they laid Jesus there.

The Resurrection

CHAPTER 20   Early on Sunday morning, while it was still dark, Mary Magdalene came to the tomb and found that the stone had been rolled away from the entrance. 2 She ran and found Simon Peter and the other disciple, the one whom Jesus loved. She said, "They have taken the Lord's body out of the tomb, and we don't know where they have put him!"

3 Peter and the other disciple started out for the tomb. 4 They were both running, but the other disciple outran Peter and reached the tomb first. 5 He stooped and looked in and saw the linen wrappings lying there, but he didn't go in. 6 Then Simon Peter arrived and went inside. He also noticed the linen wrappings lying there, 7 while the cloth that had covered Jesus' head was folded up and lying apart from the other

FYI

 How had Nicodemus changed from his encounter with Jesus in chapter 3?

In what ways are some people "secret disciples" of Jesus today? What might they be afraid of?

 Describe one way you have been changed (like Nicodemus) because of knowing and following Jesus.

Joseph and Nicodemus were secret followers. When Jesus was alive, they sneaked around to learn from him. But when he died, they honored him with costly gifts. Do you think Joseph and Nicodemus regretted not going public before then? Think of how much more they could have learned. Jesus, give us the courage to go public with our faith in you.

Dear God — Thank you for the people who loved and served Jesus after his death. Please help me love and serve the living Jesus every day.

wrappings. 8 Then the disciple who had reached the tomb first also went in, and he saw and believed– 9 for until then they still hadn't understood the Scriptures that said Jesus must rise from the dead. 10 Then they went home.

11 Mary was standing outside the tomb crying, and as she wept, she stooped and looked in. 12 She saw two white-robed angels, one sitting at the head and the other at the foot of the place where the body of Jesus had been lying. 13 "Dear woman, why are you crying?" the angels asked her.

"Because they have taken away my Lord," she replied, "and I don't know where they have put him."

14 She turned to leave and saw someone standing there. It was Jesus, but she didn't recognize him. 15 *"Dear woman, why are you crying?"* Jesus asked her. *"Who are you looking for?"*

She thought he was the gardener. "Sir," she said, "if you have taken him away, tell me where you have put him, and I will go and get him."

16 *"Mary!"* Jesus said.

She turned to him and cried out, "Rabboni!" (which is Hebrew for "Teacher").

17 *"Don't cling to me,"* Jesus said, *"for I haven't yet ascended to the Father. But go find my brothers and tell them, 'I am ascending to my Father and your Father, to my God and your God.'"*

18 Mary Magdalene found the disciples and told them, "I have seen the Lord!" Then she gave them his message.

19 That Sunday evening the disciples were meeting behind locked doors because they were afraid of the Jewish leaders. Suddenly, Jesus was standing there among them! *"Peace be with you,"* he said. 20 As he spoke, he showed them the wounds in his hands and his side. They were filled with joy when they saw the Lord! 21 Again he said, *"Peace be with you. As the Father has sent me, so I am sending you."* 22 Then he breathed on them and said, *"Receive the Holy Spirit. 23 If you forgive anyone's sins, they are forgiven. If you do not forgive them, they are not forgiven."*

24 One of the twelve disciples, Thomas (nicknamed the Twin), was not with the others when Jesus came. 25 They told him, "We have seen the Lord!"

FYI

 Why do you think Mary didn't recognize Jesus at first?

Why do you think Jesus emphasized the idea of "my Father and your Father, my God and your God" in verse 17?

Why do you think the disciples were afraid of the religious leaders? How do you think you might feel in the same situation? Why?

 Write out verse 22 here. Spend some time thinking about the Holy Spirit, the breath of Jesus.

Mary saw Jesus with her own eyes, and she heard his voice as he asked her a question. Overwhelmed by grief, she didn't realize that it was the risen Christ standing in front of her. Then she heard Jesus call her by name, "Mary." In that moment, she recognized the voice of the Lord who loved her. May we be quick to recognize the voice of Jesus who loves us and calls us by name.

Dear God — Thank you for the miracle of Jesus' resurrection. Thank you that we follow a living Savior. Thank you for the gift of Jesus' peace and the Holy Spirit.

But he replied, "I won't believe it unless I see the nail wounds in his hands, put my fingers into them, and place my hand into the wound in his side."

26 Eight days later the disciples were together again, and this time Thomas was with them. The doors were locked; but suddenly, as before, Jesus was standing among them. *"Peace be with you,"* he said. 27 Then he said to Thomas, *"Put your finger here, and look at my hands. Put your hand into the wound in my side. Don't be faithless any longer. Believe!"*

28 "My Lord and my God!" Thomas exclaimed.

29 Then Jesus told him, *"You believe because you have seen me. Blessed are those who believe without seeing me."*

Purpose of the Book

30 The disciples saw Jesus do many other miraculous signs in addition to the ones recorded in this book. 31 But these are written so that you may continue to believe that Jesus is the Messiah, the Son of God, and that by believing in him you will have life by the power of his name.

Epilogue: Jesus Appears to Seven Disciples

CHAPTER 21 Later, Jesus appeared again to the disciples beside the Sea of Galilee. This is how it happened. 2 Several of the disciples were there—Simon Peter, Thomas (nicknamed the Twin), Nathanael from Cana in Galilee, the sons of Zebedee, and two other disciples.

3 Simon Peter said, "I'm going fishing."

"We'll come, too," they all said. So they went out in the boat, but they caught nothing all night.

4 At dawn Jesus was standing on the beach, but the disciples couldn't see who he was. 5 He called out, *"Fellows, have you caught any fish?"*

"No," they replied.

6 Then he said, *"Throw out your net on the right-hand side of the boat, and you'll get some!"* So they did, and they couldn't haul in the net because there were so many fish in it.

7 Then the disciple Jesus loved said to Peter, "It's the Lord!" When Simon Peter heard that it was the Lord, he put on his tunic (for he had stripped for work), jumped into the water, and headed to shore.

FYI

The sons of Zebedee were James and John.

The disciple Jesus loved was John, who wrote this account of Jesus' life.

 What do you think about Thomas's doubts and questions?

According to John 20:31, John wrote the book so people would "believe that Jesus is the Messiah, the Son of God." How has John's book impacted your belief and faith in Jesus?

Why do you think the prologue (chapter 21) is included in John?

 Write here some reasons why you believe the Jesus is the Messiah, the King, the Son of God, your Savior.

We all need power — power for our phones, power for our vehicles, power for our gaming devices, power for our computers. Do you want power for your life? If so, tap into that power by believing that Jesus Christ is your King (the Messiah), echoing Thomas's words that Jesus is "My Lord and my God!" If you do that, you will absolutely have life now and forever — life that never ends, and power that never runs out.

Dear God — Thank you for the written record of Jesus' life. Help me listen to it, learn from it, and grow closer to Jesus through it.

8 The others stayed with the boat and pulled the loaded net to the shore, for they were only about a hundred yards from shore. 9 When they got there, they found breakfast waiting for them—fish cooking over a charcoal fire, and some bread. 10 *"Bring some of the fish you've just caught,"* Jesus said. 11 So Simon Peter went aboard and dragged the net to the shore. There were 153 large fish, and yet the net hadn't torn.

12 *"Now come and have some breakfast!"* Jesus said. None of the disciples dared to ask him, "Who are you?" They knew it was the Lord. 13 Then Jesus served them the bread and the fish. 14 This was the third time Jesus had appeared to his disciples since he had been raised from the dead.

15 After breakfast Jesus asked Simon Peter, *"Simon son of John, do you love me more than these?"*

"Yes, Lord," Peter replied, "you know I love you."

"Then feed my lambs," Jesus told him.

16 Jesus repeated the question: *"Simon son of John, do you love me?"*

"Yes, Lord," Peter said, "you know I love you."

"Then take care of my sheep," Jesus said.

17 A third time he asked him, *"Simon son of John, do you love me?"*

Peter was hurt that Jesus asked the question a third time. He said, "Lord, you know everything. You know that I love you."

Jesus said, *"Then feed my sheep.*

18 *"I tell you the truth, when you were young, you were able to do as you liked; you dressed yourself and went wherever you wanted to go. But when you are old, you will stretch out your hands, and others will dress you and take you where you don't want to go."* 19 Jesus said this to let him know by what kind of death he would glorify God. Then Jesus told him, *"Follow me."*

20 Peter turned around and saw behind them the disciple Jesus loved—the one who had leaned over to Jesus during supper and asked, "Lord, who will betray you?" 21 Peter asked Jesus, "What about him, Lord?"

22 Jesus replied, *"If I want him to remain alive until I return, what is that to you? As for you, follow me."* 23 So the rumor spread among the community of believers that this disciple wouldn't die. But that isn't what Jesus said at all. He only said, *"If I want him to remain alive until I return, what is that to you?"*

Why do you think Jesus asked Peter the same question three times?

What do you think Jesus meant when he told Peter to "feed my sheep"?

List the names of people who have "fed" and cared for you spiritually, like Jesus told Peter to do. Thank God for these people. Think of a way to personally thank those people.

When Jesus came back to life, he was a new kind of human being who could appear suddenly in locked rooms. But he was also a familiar kind of human being who made campfires, cooked breakfast for his friends, and had casual conversations. We serve and love Jesus, who is both glorious and God, personal and human. He is everything, forever and ever. Amen.

Dear God —— Thank you for bringing people into my life who love Jesus and teach me about him. Help me to learn from them and to grow deeper in my love for you.

24 This disciple is the one who testifies to these events

and has recorded them here.

And we know that his account of these things is accurate.

25 Jesus also did many other things. If they were all written down,

I suppose the whole world could not contain

the books that would be written.

Made in United States
Orlando, FL
09 February 2022

14637875R00059